Presented To:

_____

From:

_____

Date:

_____

God's Little
Devotional Book
on
PRAYER

*My sister Irene gave me this book.
I love my sister Irene.
"Thank you Irene".
2023 March 27.*

Tulsa, Oklahoma

God's Little Devotional Book on Prayer
ISBN 1-56292-266-1
Copyright © 1997 by Honor Books, Inc.
P. O. Box 55388
Tulsa, Oklahoma 74155

3rd Printing

Manuscript compiled by W. B. Freeman Concepts, Inc.,
Tulsa, Oklahoma.

God's Little
Devotional Book
on
PRAYER

INTRODUCTION

> It's me, it's me, it's me, O Lord,
> Standin' in the need of prayer.
> Not my brother, not my sister...
> Not my father, not my mother...
> Not my preacher, not my deacon...
> but it's me, O Lord,
> standin' in the need of prayer.

The words of this traditional spiritual point to a deep-seated, basic need in each of our hearts: the need for God. Every human being was born with the desire to have an intimate relationship with Him, so that we might draw from His infinite power and love all that we, as finite beings, need and desire.

Since our communication with Him — the means by which we acknowledge our needs and request His assistance — is forged in prayer, we *need* to pray. Not only do we need to pray privately for our own needs to be met, but we need for pray for others and with others.

In its simplest form, prayer is talking things over with God. He is always ready to hear anything we are willing to share. We need not use lofty "Thee-and-Thou" type language, but speak to Him in plain terms, the same way we would speak to our closest friend. Furthermore, we can pray wherever we may be, in whatever position, at whatever time, for whatever purpose, and about whatever situation. He is eager to hear from us! He desires to share all of Himself with us.

The devotions in this book are intended to guide you in *how* to pray and encourage you *to* pray. This is not just another book to teach you more about prayer, although you will learn more, its purpose is to motivate you to actually pray. Prayer is understood best by those who practice it. Prayer is an experience, not a theory.

We often conclude our prayers with the word, "Amen," which literally means, "may it be so." Today, in encouraging your *active* prayer life, we say to you... *Amen!*

Beware of placing the emphasis on what prayer costs us; it cost God everything to make it possible for us to pray.

■ ■ ■

*Since therefore, brethren, we have
confidence to enter the holy place
by the blood of Jesus...let us
draw near with a sincere heart
in full assurance of faith.*

Hebrews 10:19,22 NASB

*D*uring the reign of Oliver Cromwell, the British government ran low on the silver they used to make their coins. Lord Cromwell sent his men to a local cathedral in search of silver. They reported, "The only silver we could find is in the statues of the saints standing in the corners." "Good!" Cromwell replied, "We'll melt down the saints and put them into circulation."[1]

Circulating melted-down saints? It's an unusual metaphor, but good theology! The Lord never intended for us to be silver-plated, highly polished ornaments solely for liturgical use. He intends for us to give our all — our very life's blood, talent, sweat, resources, time, and yes, silver — to wage war against the evil out in the trenches of life.

A man once prayed, "Lord, I want to be Your man, so I give You my money, my car, and my home." Then he added, "I bet it's been a while since someone gave so much." The Lord replied, "No. Not really."[2]

The Lord wants far more than our material possessions. He wants our hearts, our prayers, our tears. He wants to be the object of our desire. The blood of Jesus can't be bought. It can only be received by nothing less than our all.

Prayer requires that
we stand in God's
presence...proclaiming
to ourselves and
to others that without
God we can do nothing.

■ ■ ■

He who abides in Me, and I in him,
bears much fruit; for without Me
you can do nothing.

John 15:5 NKJV

$\mathcal{A}$ man once asked Dwight L. Moody, "How can you accept the Bible with all its mysteries and contradictions, you with your fine mind?"

Moody replied, "I don't explain it. I don't understand it. I don't make anything of it. I simply believe it."

In his classic book, *Prayer,* Dr. O. Hallesby echoed this attitude. He wrote, "Prayer and helplessness are inseparable. Only he who is helpless can truly pray.... Prayer (therefore) consists simply in telling God day by day in what ways we feel helpless. We are moved to pray every time the Spirit of God, which is the Spirit of prayer, emphasizes anew to us our helplessness, and we realize how impotent we are by nature to believe, to love, to hope, to serve, to sacrifice, to suffer, to read the Bible, to pray, and to struggle against our sinful desires."[3]

God isn't looking for your perfection and your strength today. He is looking for you to trust in His perfection and His strength.

Prayer is profitable wherever it is invested.

■ ■ ■

Then Jonah prayed unto the Lord his God out of the fish's belly.

Jonah 2:1

A minister and his wife were once met at a train station by a woman who had been assigned to drive them to their hotel. As they approached the center of town, the traffic was very heavy. "You can let us off at the nearest corner," the minister suggested, certain she would never find a parking space close to their hotel.

"No trouble," she said. Then she began to pray, "God, we really need a parking space. If one is nearby, please lead me to it." She drove around the block a couple of times, then just as they turned the corner a car pulled out of a parking space right in front of their hotel. She said sincerely, "Thanks, God. I really appreciate this!"

The minister's wife asked the woman if she always asked God for such favors. She answered, "Oh, yes. I chatter to God all the time. I can't help it. He seems to be so close that I talk to Him just the way I'd talk to my best friend."[4]

God delights in meeting our small needs just as much as our big ones — the same as any loving friend or father. All prayer, and all answers to prayer, build our relationship with God. And a deep personal relationship — marked by ongoing, free-flowing communication — is what God desires to have with each one of us.

I know not by
what methods rare,
But this I know:
God answers prayer.

■ ■ ■

*Then you shall call, and the Lord
will answer; you shall cry for help,
and he will say, Here I am.*

Isaiah 58:9 NRSV

Soon after Dallas Theological Seminary opened in 1924, it faced a major financial crisis. Creditors banded together and announced that they intended to foreclose. On the morning of the threatened foreclosure, the leadership of the seminary met in the president's office to pray that God would meet their need. One of the men present was Harry Ironside, who prayed in his characteristic style, "Lord, the cattle on a thousand hills are Thine. Please sell some of them and send us the money."

While they were praying, a tall Texan walked into the outer office and said to the secretary, "I just sold two carloads of cattle. I've been trying to make a business deal but it fell through, and I feel compelled to give the money to the seminary. I don't know if you need it, but here's the check."

Knowing the financial need, the secretary took the check and timidly tapped on the door of the office where the prayer meeting was being held. When Dr. Chafer saw the check, he was amazed. The gift was *exactly* the amount of the debt! Recognizing the name on the check as that of a prominent Ft. Worth cattleman. He announced with joy, "Harry, God sold the cattle!"[5]

The best advice my mother ever gave me — don't forget to say your prayers.

■ ■ ■

Therefore let everyone who is godly pray to you while you may be found; surely when the mighty waters rise, they will not reach him.

Psalm 32:6 NIV

Sandra Goodwin's poem, "Traveling On My Knees" reminds us that prayer is the generator for God's power at work in our world. When we fail to pray, because He desires to release His will in the world through our prayers, less is accomplished in God's kingdom!

Last night I took a journey to a land across the seas;

I did not go by boat or plane, I traveled on my knees.

I saw so many people there in deepest depths of sin.

But Jesus told me I should go, that there were souls to win.

But I said, "Jesus, I cannot go and work with such as these." He answered quickly, "Yes, you can by traveling on your knees."

He said, "You pray; I'll meet the need, you call and I will hear; be concerned about lost souls, of those both far and near."

And so I tried it, knelt in prayer, gave up some hours of ease; I felt the Lord right by my side while traveling on my knees.

As I prayed on I saw souls saved and twisted bodies healed, and saw God's workers' strength renewed while laboring on the fields.

I said, "Yes, Lord, I have a job, my desire Thy will to please; I can go and heed Thy call by traveling on my knees."[6]

Prayer is a direct link to peace of mind and perspective. It reminds us of who we are.

■ ■ ■

Trust in the Lord with all your heart and lean not on your own understanding; in all your ways acknowledge him, and he will make your paths straight.

Proverbs 3:5,6 NIV

$\mathcal{A}$ church once sent a man to spend two months as a volunteer at Mother Teresa's mission in Calcutta, caring for India's sick, poor, and dying. He left on his mission with great joy — the trip was a dream come true.

Standing by a luggage carousel in Bangkok, forty hours later, he felt anything but elation. Somewhere between South Korea and Thailand his luggage had been "misdirected." Nerves worn raw by sleeplessness, he collapsed into a nearby chair and wondered, *Was this trip a mistake?* He felt as lost as his bags.

As his eyes wandered around the walls of the lobby, which was mostly empty owing to the late hour, he noticed a row of clocks on one wall. They displayed the time in London, New York, Sydney, and Bangkok. He quickly noted that it was noon at his home church — and it was Sunday.

His church had promised to pray for him at noon services that day. *They're praying for me right now*, he thought. And with that realization came a tremendous peace. *I'm not alone now. And I won't be alone in the months ahead!*[7]

Luggage may often be misdirected, but not our prayers. God knows your need and He knows where you are.

True prayer is a way of life, not just in case of emergency.

■ ■ ■

*And pray in the Spirit
on all occasions with all kinds
of prayers and requests.*
Ephesians 6:18 NIV

*I*n *Who Is for Life?* Mother Teresa writes about the link between love and prayer — both of which must find daily expression:

"Let us pray for each other so that we grow in tender love, that we allow God to love us, and that we allow God to love others through us....

"I will never forget that I once met a man in the street who looked very lonely and miserable. So I walked right up to him, and I shook his hand. My hands were always very warm; and he looked up, gave me a beautiful smile, and he said, 'Oh, it has been such a long, long time since I felt the warmth of a human hand!' How very wonderful and very beautiful that our simple actions can show love in that way.

"And let us remember to bring that kind of love into our family. We can do this through prayer; for where there is prayer, there is love. And where there is love, there is the complete oneness that Jesus was talking about when He said, 'Be one, as the Father and I are one. And love one another as I love you. As the Father has loved me, I have loved you.'"[8]

When you pray for your family and friends — and even your enemies — you are expressing love. When you express love to those same people though your actions, you are living out your prayers in your way of life.

We should never pray without reading the Bible, and we should never read the Bible without praying.

■ ■ ■

For the reverence and fear of God are basic to all wisdom. Knowing God results in every other kind of understanding.

Proverbs 9:10 TLB

*D*r. Alexander Maclaren is considered one of the clearest Bible expositors of his time. He attributed becoming such a great Bible scholar to a habit he had, which he never broke: spending one hour a day "alone with the Eternal."

The hour which Dr. Maclaren designated was from nine to ten in the morning. At times, he allowed others into his prayer closet, but they were never allowed to utter a word. Maclaren would sit in his well-worn armchair, with his big Bible laying across his knees. Sometimes he would read its pages, but most often he would just sit with his hand over his face.

During that hour he did not allow himself to read the Bible as a student, or to search for texts to use in sermons or lessons. One of his assistants noted, "he read the Bible as a child would read a letter from an absent father, as a loving heart would drink in again the message from a loved one far away."[9]

When we pray, we open our hearts to a clearer and deeper understanding of God's Word. As we read His Word, we open our minds to a greater understanding of how and for what to pray.

I do not always
bend the knee to pray;
I often pray in
crowded city street
in some hard crisis
of a busy day — prayer
is my sure and
comforting retreat.

■ ■ ■

Be merciful unto me, O Lord:
for I cry unto thee daily.
Psalm 86:3

*I*n an article for *America* magazine titled, "Praying in a Time of Depression," Jane Redmont wrote:

"On a quick trip to New York for a consulting job, a week or two into the anti-depressant drug and feeling no relief, I fell into a seven-hour anxiety attack with recurring suicidal ideations. On the morning after my arrival I found I could not focus my attention; yet focus was crucial in the job I was contracted to do for 24 hours, as recorder and process observer at a conference of urban activists that was beginning later that day. I felt as if I were about to jump out of my skin — or throw myself under a truck.

"An hour away from the beginning of the conference, walking uptown on a noisy Manhattan street in the afternoon, I prayed...perhaps out loud, I am not sure. I said with all my strength, 'Jesus, I don't usually ask You for much, but I am asking You now, in the name of all those people whom You healed, in the name of the man born blind and the bent-over woman and the woman who bled for years, in the name of the man with the demons and the little girl whom You raised up, *help me.*'

"Within an hour, I was calm again."[10]

God is our high tower, a refuge in times of trouble. We can pray in the midst of anxiety and depression and God will fill us with His peace that passes understanding, sheltering us from the torment of our worry and restoring us once again.

Here at my office desk
I ask His aid, no matter
where I am I crave His
care; in moments when
my soul is sore afraid it
comforts most to know
He's everywhere.

Seek the Lord and his strength,
seek his face continually.

1 Chronicles 16:11

$\mathcal{H}$ave you ever explored a tidal pool? Low tide is the perfect time to find a myriad of creatures that have temporarily washed ashore from the depths of the sea.

Children are often amazed that they can pick up these shelled creatures and stare at them eyeball to eyeball. The creatures rarely exhibit any form of overt fear, such as moving to attack or attempting to scurry away. Usually, the children are the ones who squeal in fear, thinking themselves exposed and vulnerable to the possibility of the creatures' bites, pinches, or stings. The creatures simply withdraw into their shells, instinctively knowing they are safe as long as they remain in their nice, strong shelters.

Likewise, we are safe when we remain in Christ. We are protected from the hassles of life, the unknowns, the bites and stings of temptation and sin. Those things will come against us, much like the fingers of a brave and curious child try to invade the sea creature's shell, but they have no power to harm us when we retreat into the shelter of Christ.

The Lord commanded us to learn to *abide* in Him and to *remain* steadfast in our faith. He tells us to *trust* in Him absolutely, and to *shelter* ourselves under His strong wings, and in the cleft of His rock-like presence. He delights when we *retreat* into His arms for comfort and tender expressions of love.

Our business in prayer is not to prescribe but to subscribe to the wisdom and will of God; to refer our case to Him, and then leave it with Him.

■ ■ ■

Commit your way to the Lord,
trust also in Him,
and He shall bring it to pass.

Psalm 37:5 NKJV

This prayer from *The Gardener's Year*, reminds us that when we tell God what to do in prayer, we are speaking from our limited, finite point of view. We are much better off when we simply state our requests, and then trust Him to respond from His eternal storehouse with His great generosity and unquestionable wisdom.

> O Lord, grant that in some way it may rain every day, say from about midnight until three o'clock in the morning, but You see, it must be gentle and warm so that it can soak in; grant that at the same time it would not rain on campion, alyssum, helianthemum, lavender, and the others which You...know are drought-loving plants — I will write their names on a bit of paper if you like — and grant that the sun may shine the whole day long, but not everywhere (not, for instance, on spiraea or on gentian, platain lily and rhododendron) and not too much; that there may be plenty of dew and little wind, enough worms, no plant-lice and snails, no mildew, and that once a week thin liquid manure and guano may fall from heaven. Amen.[11]

The prayer that begins
with trustfulness, and
passes on into waiting,
will always end in
thankfulness, triumph,
and praise.

■■■

*Elijah was a man with a nature like
ours, and he prayed earnestly that it
might not rain; and it did not rain.*

James 5:17 NASB

A mother was awakened one night to hear the news that her son, who was away at college, had fallen and was seriously injured. As she and her husband raced to the hospital, she prayed over and over again, "Dear God, please let our son be all right." The doctor greeted them with grim news. Their son had injured his spinal cord in the fall and would be permanently paralyzed from the neck down.

The mother thought it would be impossible for her son to finish college, but he remained determined to do so. Within three months after his hospitalization and rehabilitation at a spinal center, he enrolled at a college near home.

His mother was concerned about how he would get around campus in a wheelchair, or take notes with the special brace he had just begun learning to use. But four years later, her son graduated with his bachelor's degree. He then went on to law school, and within three years, received his law degree. He passed the bar exam and began to work for a law firm.

She has said about her experience, "No, God didn't answer my prayers in the way I had thought He would...[my son] had to struggle, but...he has done more than all right!"[12]

When we serve the Lord
with our whole heart,
we have confidence
and joy in prayer.

■ ■ ■

*We receive from Him whatever we ask
for, because we (watchfully) obey His
orders...and (habitually) practice
what is pleasing to Him.*

1 John 3:22 AMP

$\mathcal{D}$r. Wilbur Chapman wrote the following letter to a friend telling him about a great lesson he had learned concerning prayer:

"At one of our missions in England the audiences were exceedingly small; but I received a note saying that an American missionary was going to pray God's blessing down on our work. He was known as Praying Hyde. Almost instantly the tide turned. The hall became packed, and at my first invitation fifty men accepted Christ as their Savior. As we were leaving I said, 'Mr. Hyde, I want you to pray for me.' He came to my room, turned the key in the door, dropped on his knees, and waited five minutes without a single syllable coming from his lips. I could hear my own heart thumping, and his beating. I felt hot tears running down my face. I knew I was with God. Then, with upturned face, down which the tears were streaming, he said, 'O God.' Then for five minutes at least he was still again; and then, when he knew that he was talking with God there came from the depths of his heart such petitions for me as I had never heard before. I rose from my knees to know what real prayer was."[13]

True prayer is voiced first in the heart.

To pray does
not only mean
to seek help;
it also means
to seek Him.

■ ■ ■

Your face, Lord, do I seek.

Psalm 27:8 NRSV

On a bitterly cold night in February of 1943, one of the great maritime losses of World War II occurred — the sinking of the *SS Dorchester* in the North Atlantic. Of the 904 men aboard, 678 lost their lives.

Clark Poling was a young chaplain assigned to the ship. Before going to sea he asked his father, Daniel A. Poling, to pray for him, but with this stipulation: pray not for his safety, but that he would be adequate for any situation. Poling prayed as his son had requested.

When the enemy's torpedo struck the Dorchester and the ship began to sink, many of the men became paralyzed with fear. Young Poling, along with three other chaplains, strapped their own life belts to the fear-stricken men. They helped load the lifeboats, and then joined hands in a circle of prayer as they sank to their watery graves. Poling's prayer had been answered. Although his son had not remained in safety, he had been adequate for the situation.[14]

Ultimately, our adequacy for any situation is found only in the Lord. He provides what we need to remain true to Him and to be His brightest light in the darkest of circumstances.

Time spent in prayer is never wasted.

■■■

Let us not grow weary
while doing good,
for in due season
we shall reap
if we do not lose heart.

Galatians 6:9 NKJV

*W*hen Jill was a little girl, she visited her grandparents' farm every summer. One day, as she came into the farmhouse she could hear her grandmother talking. She entered the living room cautiously, certain that her grandmother had company. Instead, she found her grandmother alone, in prayer. Jill felt as if she was treading on holy ground.

As she quietly made her way toward the staircase, she was amazed to hear her name. Her grandmother was praying for her! She listened intently as her grandmother pleaded with God to keep her safe and healthy, and to give her a desire to follow the Lord and grow up to be a soulwinner. Tears sprang to Jill's eyes as she felt the love expressed in her grandmother's prayer.

A few years later when Jill was in high school, a friend invited her to attend a youth rally. That evening, she gave her life to Christ. Later that night, she recalled the prayers of her grandmother. She suddenly realized, tears flowing down her face — *My grandmother's prayer has been answered!* The answer had taken nearly a decade to manifest, but nevertheless, the answer had come — not only for her grandmother, but for Jill.

God knows the seasons of our hearts. Our role is to persist in prayer — planting seeds and watering them — until we reap the harvest!

By far the most important thing about praying is to keep at it.

■ ■ ■

Then Jesus told them a parable about their need to pray always and not to lose heart.

Luke 18:1 NRSV

$\mathcal{A}$ man who owned a plot of land was about to leave the area on a journey that would take several years. Before he left, he leased his land to others. When he returned, he discovered his renters had been very careless and brambles had sprung up, turning his plot of land into a wilderness of thorns. Desiring to cultivate the land, he said to his son, "Your next job is to go and clear that ground."

The son visited the acreage and quickly concluded, *It will take forever to get this land cleared!* Overwhelmed by the idea, he lay on the ground and went to sleep. He did the same day after day. When his father came to see what had been done, he found his son asleep and the land untouched.

When his father woke him, the son complained that the job had looked so monumental, he could never make himself begin to tackle the project. His father replied, "Son, if you had only cleared the area on which you lay down for a nap each day, your work would have advanced and you would not have lost heart." After the father left, the son began to do what his father had advised. In a short time, the plot of land was cleared and cultivated.[15]

Daily prayer clears away the brambles in our hearts. Don't give up! God is working something good in *you*...prayer by prayer!

The most praying souls are the most assured souls.

■ ■ ■

*The Lord is righteous
in all his ways...He fulfills
the desires of those who fear him;
he hears their cry and saves them.*

Psalm 145:17,19 NIV

*O*n a remote farm in California, a young mother was alone with her three children. The children had been swimming in the family pool when the mother suddenly noticed that her two-and-a-half-year-old son was at the bottom of it. She dove in and pulled him out as quickly as she could.

Just at that moment, a neighboring farmer came by. He immediately began careful mouth-to-mouth resuscitation. After several minutes, the child stirred. The mother and the farmer took him to the nearest hospital for examination, and the doctors assured them that the little boy had suffered no brain damage.

In the days following, as people heard of the child's rescue, several commented to the mother and father, "You sure were lucky!" The father said to his pastor, "When people said that to me, I replied, 'It wasn't luck at all. My wife and daughter were on their knees praying while the farmer was working on my son.'"[16]

Those who pray can always be assured that God is at work in their particular circumstance — for their eternal benefit.

Prayer crowns God with the honor and glory due to His name, and God crowns prayer with assurance and comfort.

■ ■ ■

I will exalt you, my God the King...and extol your name for ever and ever. Great is the Lord and most worthy of praise; his greatness no one can fathom.

Psalm 145:1-3 NIV

*I*magine for a moment that someone you love comes to you and asks to borrow a small sum of money. You no doubt would lend it gladly, in part because of the close relationship you share.

Now imagine that this same person continues to come to you, asking for loans, food, clothing, the use of your car, a place to stay, and to borrow tools and appliances. While you do love this person, you would probably begin to feel that something was wrong. It's not the asking, but the attitude.

What causes the change in this type of situation? The person who is coming with requests no longer sees his friend as someone whose feelings can be hurt, but as a source of goods and services. From the perspective of the one who is giving, the friend with whom dreams and innermost thoughts have been shared is now perceived as being concerned only with getting his own needs met.

So often we come to God in prayer with our request list in hand — "God, please do this..." or "God, I want...." We are wise to reconsider our relationship with God in prayer. Who is this One to whom we pray? How good has He been to us? How much does He deserve our praise and thanksgiving?

Although we can't hurt God's feelings, we are missing out on an intimate relationship with Him when we always come with an empty hand, instead of a heart full of praise and thanksgiving.

God looks not at the oratory of your prayers, how elegant they may be; nor at the geometry of your prayers, how long they may be; nor at the arithmetic of your prayers, how many they may be; nor at the logic of your prayers, how methodical they may be; but the sincerity of them.

■ ■ ■

*In Christ we speak
as persons of sincerity.*
2 Corinthians 2:17 NRSV

*T*hree ministers were talking about prayer one day, and they began debating among themselves the most appropriate and effective positions for prayer. As they talked, they were totally oblivious of a telephone repairman working on the phone system in a corner of the room where they were sitting.

One minister contended that the key to prayer was in the hands. He always held his hands together to show a firmness of commitment and then pointed his hands upward as a symbolic form of worship. The second minister countered, real prayer could only be made if a person was on his knees. That, to him, was the proper position for submission to God. The third suggested that the very best position for prayer was to pray while stretched out flat on one's face, the position of supreme surrender.

By this time, the telephone repairman could no longer refrain from adding his opinion: "Well, I have found that the most powerful prayer I ever made was while I was suspended forty feet above the ground dangling upside down by my heels from a telephone pole."[17]

The real power of prayer lies in the One who hears our prayers, not in the form of the prayer.

The fewer words the better prayer.

■ ■ ■

And when you pray, do not use vain repetitions as the heathen do. For they think that they will be heard for their many words. Therefore do not be like them.

Matthew 6:7,8 NKJV

"*D*ad," a little boy once asked, "does the Lord know everything?"

"Yes, son," the father replied. The boy nodded, but didn't look very convinced, prompting the father to ask a question of his own, "Why do you ask?"

"Because," the boy replied, "when the preacher prays, he prays so long telling God everything, that I thought maybe God wasn't clued in on what's happening to folks around here."

God is much more concerned about our motives than in the type, amount, or form of the words we use in prayer. He looks on the heart. Sometimes a simple SOS is all that is required.

One Sunday morning as the great preacher Charles H. Spurgeon passed through the door on his way to the pulpit, he was overwhelmed by the great crowd of people who had already gathered for the service. As strong in faith and as profound and experienced a preacher as he was, an assistant overheard him pray simply, "O God, help!" Spurgeon's prayer needed no elaboration. And often, ours don't either.

Prayer is the chief
agency and activity
whereby men
align themselves
with God's purpose.

■ ■ ■

We know that all things work together
for good for those who love God, who
are called according to his purpose.

Romans 8:28 NRSV

*W*hen David Dorr, the husband of Roberta Dorr, author of the novel *Bathsheba*, was a surgical resident, he was told that he had Hodgkins disease. David accepted the verdict of a limited life span and went about his work. Roberta responded differently. "Why?" she asked God, but no answer came.

Finally, in total relinquishment, she asked God, "How do You want me to pray for my husband?" She soon felt this strong impression: "Pray that your husband will be able to use for the good of others the medical training he has been given." As soon as she prayed this prayer, the heavy burden lifted from her heart. She felt she was praying *God's* prayer, sharing His concern for all of humanity.

A year later during a periodic test, the doctors at Johns Hopkins were astonished to find no trace of disease in David. Three years later they dismissed him entirely, unable to explain what had happened. David completed his residency and went to the Gaza Strip where he was desperately needed as a surgeon.[18]

To pray God's will we first must discover what His will is. All we must do is ask. He *will* answer.

Prayer is not only
"the practice of the
presence of God,"
it is the realization
of His presence.

■ ■ ■

*Thou wilt make known to me the path
of life; in Thy presence is fulness of joy.*

Psalm 16:11 NASB

In A Slow and Certain Light, Elisabeth Elliot writes: "When I lived in the forest of Ecuador I usually traveled on foot.... Trails often led through streams and rivers which we had to wade, but sometimes there was a log high above the water which we had to cross.

"I dreaded those logs and was always tempted to take the steep, hard way down into the ravine and up the other side. But the Indians would say, 'Just walk across, señorita,' and over they would go, light-footed and confident. I was barefoot as they were, but it was not enough. On the log, I couldn't keep from looking down at the river below. I knew I would slip. I had never been any good at balancing myself...so my guide would stretch out a hand, and the touch of it was all I needed. I stopped worrying about slipping. I stopped looking down at the river or even at the log and looked at the guide, who held my hand with only the lightest touch. When I reached the other side, I realized that if I had slipped he could not have held me. But his being there and his touch were all I needed."[19]

A major source of comfort in prayer is simply realizing that God *is* present.

No Christian is greater than his prayer life.

■ ■ ■

When they saw the courage of Peter and John and realized that they were unschooled, ordinary men, they were astonished and they took note that these men had been with Jesus.

Acts 4:13 NIV

*I*n the early days of the formation of the United States, a stranger once asked how he might identify George Washington among those present at Congress. He was told, "You can easily distinguish him when Congress goes to prayer. Washington is the gentleman who kneels."

Washington had a long-standing reputation as a man of prayer. At Valley Forge, he frequently found rest and relief in prayer. One day a farmer approaching the military camp heard an earnest voice. When he drew nearer, he saw Washington on his knees, his cheeks wet with tears. The farmer returned home and said to his wife: "George Washington will succeed! George Washington will succeed! The Americans will secure their independence!"

"What makes you think so, Isaac?" his wife asked. The farmer replied, "I heard him pray, Hannah, out in the woods today, and the Lord will surely hear his prayer. He will, Hannah; thee may rest assured He will."

One person, willing to humble himself and pray can leave a legacy of faith and hope, giving courage to future generations.

The first purpose of prayer is to know God.

■ ■ ■

I lift up my eyes to the hills —
where does my help come from?
My help comes from the Lord,
the Maker of heaven and earth.

Psalm 121:1,2 NIV

A house party once was held in an English manor. As was customary, the after-dinner entertainment featured recitations and songs from the guests. A famous actor was present, and when it came his turn to perform, he recited the Twenty-third Psalm. His rendition of the familiar psalm was magnificent and received with much applause.

Later in the evening, the hostess noticed her little old great-aunt dozing in the corner of the room. She was almost completely deaf and had missed most of the evening's entertainment. Still, the other guests urged her to recite something. Since most people of that era knew many poems by memory, the hostess felt sure she would recite a poem. To everyone's surprise, she stood up, her voice quivering, and recited the Twenty-third Psalm! When she finished there were tears in most eyes, including those of the famous actor. One of the guests later approached the actor and said, "You recited that psalm absolutely superbly. It was incomparable. So why were we so moved by that funny, little old lady?"

He replied, "I know the psalm. She knows the Shepherd."

Prayer is our foremost way of getting better acquainted with Him.

As artists give
themselves to their
models, and poets to
their classical pursuits,
so must we addict
ourselves to prayer.

■ ■ ■

Devote yourselves to prayer,
keeping alert in it with
an attitude of thanksgiving.
Colossians 4:2 NASB

A father was playing ball with his young son one day when his son's best friend appeared in the backyard. "Dad, can I go play with my friend?" the boy asked.

"But son," the father replied, "we're playing ball. Don't you want to play with me?" His son replied candidly, "Nah, I'd rather play with him."

The father went inside to nurse his wounded ego, and suddenly realized that perhaps God felt the same way about his reactions at times. God jealously desires our affection and attention. The father had to admit that all too often, he had a greater interest in cars, television, yard work, sports, hobbies, books, and family activities than in spending time with God.

One of the best ways of determining addictions in our lives is to ask ourselves these two questions:

1. What is the first thing I think about in the morning?

2. What is the main thing I want to make sure is included in my day tomorrow?[20]

These are good questions to ask about our relationship with the Lord! If God were to examine your heart today, what rivals for His attention and affection would He encounter?

He who fails to pray
does not cheat God.
He cheats himself.

Blessed is the man who reveres God,
but the man who doesn't care
is headed for serious trouble.

Proverbs 28:14 TLB

𝒯or many years, it has been as common for Christians to give thanks before meals as it has been for them to eat.

During the Thirty Years' War, several Protestant officers were hiding together in a cave. Every day, a little girl from the nearest farm was sent to bring them provisions.

One day a stranger who happened to be walking through the woods joined the officers. Naturally, they were suspicious of him, but he talked so much like one of them that their doubts were overcome.

When the little farm girl came with their supplies, they offered to share their food with the stranger. To their surprise he began to eat without giving thanks. That single omission revealed the true character of the man. He was what they had suspected at the first — a spy! They barely escaped he and his comrades.[21]

When we fail to pray, we deny ourselves access to God's presence and power. We also cheat ourselves out of our identity with Christ, and deny ourselves the reputation of a faithful follower.

If you would have God
hear you when you pray,
you must hear Him
when He speaks.

*I would know the words which he
would answer me, and understand
what he would say unto me.*

Job 23:5

One day, an old woman went to Anthony Bloom and told him that while she had constantly recited the prayer of Jesus for many years, she had never really experienced the presence of God.

Bloom replied, "How can God get a word in edgeways if you never stop talking? Give him a chance. Keep quiet."

"How can I do that?" she asked. He then gave her this advice, which he subsequently gave to many others. He advised her to tidy her room each day after breakfast, making it as pleasant as possible. Then, to sit down in a position where she could see the entire room, including the window that looked out on the garden. "When you have sat down, rest for a quarter of an hour in the presence of God, but take care not to pray," Bloom said. "Be as quiet as you can and as you obviously can't do *nothing,* knit before the Lord and tell me what happens." She returned several days later, happy to report that at long last she had felt the presence of God![22]

The Lord speaks in a still, small voice; therefore, it takes a still, quiet heart to hear Him. (See 1 Kings 19:11-13.)

The value of persistent prayer is not that He will hear us...but that we will finally hear Him.

Incline your ear, and come to Me. Hear, and your soul shall live.

Isaiah 55:3 NKJV

*A*t times, we are tempted to think that because we are Christians, read our Bibles, and know a great deal *about* God, that we *know* God. The truth is that the only way we can know God is by *experiencing Him*. Many of those experiences come in prayer. As we listen quietly, we can truly hear God's whispering in our hearts.

Soren Kierkegäard noted that most of us are "so busy," we are unwilling to wait patiently for God. We might consider an appointment with a hair dresser to be inviolable, but when God lays claim to our time, we balk. Rather than spend time with God and allow ourselves to bask in His presence and soak up His love, we manufacture substitutes: things to *do* to take the place of simply *being* with Him. We offer praise, do good works, memorize Bible verses — all good activities, but unequal to resting quietly before Him.[23]

The highest value of prayer is found in developing a relationship with God. That takes both our time and our willingness to receive from Him. There is no substitute for either.

Prayer is a rising up and a drawing near to God in mind, and in heart, and in spirit.

■ ■ ■

*Draw near to God
and He will draw near to you.*

James 4:8 NASB

In Too Busy Not To Pray, Bill Hybels admits, "Prayer has not always been my strong suit. For many years, even as senior pastor of a large church, I *knew* more about prayer than I ever *practiced* in my own life. I have a racehorse temperament, and the tugs of self-sufficiency and self-reliance are very real to me. I didn't want to get off the fast track long enough to find out what prayer is all about.

"Several years ago the Holy Spirit gave me a leading so direct that I couldn't ignore it, argue against it, or disobey it. The leading was to explore, study, and practice prayer until I finally understood it." Hybels read books on prayer and studied every passage in the Bible on prayer. And then, he says, "I did something absolutely radical: I prayed."

"The greatest fulfillment in my prayer life has not been the list of miraculous answers to prayers I have received, although that has been wonderful. The greatest thrill has been the qualitative difference in my relationship with God."[24]

Are you on a casual, pray-on-the-run basis with your Creator? Or do you know His heart, sense His desires, and feel His presence? The key to ultimate fellowship with God lies in prayer.

As breath is to the body, prayer is to the soul.

■ ■ ■

*I called upon thy name, O Lord...
hide not thine ear at my breathing.*

Lamentations 3:55,56

*L*ouis Harris, the pollster, was playing tennis one day when he was struck by sharp pains in both calves. Within moments, both legs were numb. Subsequent medical tests revealed that the problem was poor circulation. Surgery was an option, but his physician preferred to try a less drastic approach first. He advised Harris to walk at least a mile every day. The doctor's hope was that as Harris' muscles demanded more blood flow, the body would bypass the clogged arteries and create new ones, called collaterals.

Harris struggled at first, but within a year, he was easily walking more than a mile a day. He has said, "I allow nothing to get in the way of my daily walk."[25]

The same must be true for our prayer life. Some might consider prayer to be an optional exercise, but in fact, prayer is vital to spiritual health. It is a channel of communication that must be kept open — unclogged and free-flowing at all times.

If we deny our souls their "recommended daily allowance" of prayer, we will over time, damage a precious and vital part of our relationship with God.

Prayer can change what arguments can't settle.

■ ■ ■

Love your enemies, bless them that curse you, do good to them that hate you, and pray for them which despitefully use you, and persecute you.

Matthew 5:44

*I*n his book, *With Justice For All*, John Perkins tells how God gave him a real compassion for white people.

The incident began when a van load of students who had participated in a civil rights march were pulled over by a highway patrolman and taken to jail. The driver of a second van called Perkins, who went to post bail for the students. No sooner had Perkins arrived at the jailhouse than he was beaten by the sheriff and tortured by several others.

He later testified in court that, although he was unconscious most of the night, he had ample opportunity to see the faces of those who had beaten him. They were faces "twisted with hate," the "victims of their own racism." Rather than hate them back, though, Perkins felt pity for them. He prayed, "God...I really want to preach a gospel that will heal these people, too."

In the months that followed, God brought the faces of numerous white people to Perkins' mind, and one by one, he forgave them. Forgiveness healed him from the wounds that had long kept him from loving whites. He wrote, "How sweet God's forgiveness and healing was!"[26]

Are you at odds with someone today? Pray for that person, so that you *both* might be healed.

If Christians spent
as much time praying
as they do grumbling,
they would soon
have nothing to
grumble about.

*Do all things without grumbling or
disputing; that you may prove
yourselves to be blameless and
innocent, children of God.*

Philippians 2:14,15 NASB

70

*U*pon hearing that the pages at his court were neglecting to ask God's blessing on their daily meals, Alfonso XII of Spain invited the boys to a banquet. He served many delicacies, which the boys ate delightedly. Not one of them, however, remembered to ask God's blessing on their food or to thank Him.

During the banquet, a dirty, ill-clad beggar entered the room. He proceeded to eat and drink to his heart's content. The pages were shocked. They expected the king to order him away, but Alfonso spoke not a word. When the beggar arose and left without so much as a word of thanks, the boys could hold back their indignation no longer. "What a despicably mean fellow!" they cried.

The king silenced them and in a calm voice said, "Boys, bolder and more audacious than this beggar have you all been. Every day you sit down to a table supplied by the bounty of your heavenly Father, yet you ask not His blessing nor express to Him your gratitude."[27]

What are you failing to give thanks for today? As you voice your "overdue" thanks, you will find that the problems you have been grumbling about will pale in comparison to God's graceful goodness.

Prayer is the wing wherewith the soul flies to heaven.

■ ■ ■

*Hear my prayer, O Lord,
and let my cry come to You.*
Psalm 102:1 NKJV

*O*ne day during her morning devotions, Jeannie found herself weeping as she read Psalm 139:23, "Search me, O God, and know my heart." She cried out to the Lord to cleanse her of several bad attitudes she had been harboring. Later that morning as she boarded an airplane, she sensed God asking her, "Are you ready?" She had a strong feeling that God was confirming to her that He had forgiven her and could now use her for a special assignment. She whispered a prayer. "Help me, Lord, to stay awake."

Jeannie usually took motion-sickness medication before flying, and therefore, often slept from takeoff to landing. On this flight, however, she forced herself to stay awake. A woman took the seat next to her on the flight and as they began to talk, the woman asked, "Why do you have so much joy?" Jeannie replied, "Jesus," and for the next three hours, she had a wonderful opportunity to witness to the woman. Later, she sent her a Bible and they exchanged letters. Then late one evening, the woman called and Jeannie led her to the Lord over the phone.[28]

The Lord will not only hear your heart's cry today, but His answer to you will bring a blessing to *your* life, *and* to the life of someone else.

If trouble drives you to prayer, prayer will drive the trouble away.

■ ■ ■

The Lord is a refuge for the oppressed, a stronghold in times of trouble.

Psalm 9:9 NIV

Shortly after Charles Colson received word that he was to be returned to Maxwell prison, he got a call from Al Quie, one of the most respected public figures in Washington. Quie said, "Chuck, I've been thinking about what else we can do to help you.... There's an old statute someone told me about. I'm going to ask the President if I can serve the rest of your term for you."

Colson was stunned. "I mean it, Chuck," Quie said. "I haven't come to this decision lightly." Overwhelmed, Colson refused his offer. Later that day, he received a note from Al Quie, who wrote, "If I could I would gladly give my life so you could use the wonderful gifts of God, that He has entrusted you with, to the glory of God...."

That night Colson completely surrendered his life: "Lord, if this is what it is all about...I praise You for giving me Your love through these men, for being God, for just letting me walk with Jesus."

Forty-eight hours later an order was issued to release Colson from prison. A Christian marshal said to him as he departed, "I kind of knew He would set you free today." Colson replied, "Thank you, but He did it two nights ago."[29]

Leave not off praying to God: for either praying will make thee leave off sinning; or continuing in sin will make thee desist from praying.

■■■

Keep watching and praying, that you may not enter into temptation; the spirit is willing, but the flesh is weak.

Matthew 26:41 NASB

"*I* just don't have time to pray" is an excuse that many of us use. This is not a new problem. As this poem from years past attests, making time for God has always been a challenge, but one worth meeting!

No time to pray!
Oh, who so fraught with earthly care.
As not to give to humble prayer
Some part of day?

No time to pray!
What heart so clean, so pure within.
That needeth not some check from sin.
Needs not to pray?

No time to pray!
'Mid each day's danger, what retreat
More needful than the mercy-seat?
Who need not pray?

No time to pray!
Then sure your record falleth short.
Excuse will fail you as resort,
On that last day.

What thought more drear,
Than that our God His face should hide,
And say through all life's swelling tide,
No time to hear![30]

—Anonymous

Do not our prayers
for help mean:
Help me to be
better than I know
myself to be.

■ ■ ■

*If we confess our sins, He is faithful
and just to forgive us our sins and to
cleanse us from all unrighteousness.*
1 John 1:9 NKJV

*W*hen Helen Keller was about six years old, her aunt made her a doll out of towels. It was a gangly, misshapen, improvised creation. The first thing Helen noticed when she picked up the doll, however, was not its shape, but that it had no eyes. She tugged at a string of beads her aunt was wearing and placed them approximately where the doll's eyes should have been. Her aunt touched Helen's eyes and then with Helen's hand in hers, touched the doll's head. Helen nodded, "yes!"

Immediately, her aunt found two buttons and sewed them onto the doll. Not being able to see herself, Helen insisted that her aunt make her doll better than she was. She wanted her doll to be "whole."[31]

Each of us instinctively desires to be whole. We know in the recesses of our hearts that we are not complete, in spite of what others tell us or what we try to tell ourselves. True wholeness comes when our entire identity is with the Lord. He alone is perfection.

Our prayers take on new intensity and meaning when we have a hunger to become like Christ. It is then that prayer becomes a path to genuine healing and wholeness. In becoming Christ-like we are always becoming better people.

Humility
is the principal
aid to prayer.

*If my people who are called
by my name humble themselves,
pray, seek my face, and turn from
their wicked ways, then I will hear
from heaven, and will forgive
their sin and heal their land.*

2 Chronicles 7:14 NRSV

*A*n Arab proverb illustrates the concept that as the tares and wheat grow, they show which God has blessed. The stalks of wheat bow their heads because God has blessed them with abundant grain. The more fruitful they are, the lower their heads. The tares lift their heads up, high above the wheat, for they are empty of grain.

D. L. Moody once said, "I have a pear tree on my farm that is very beautiful; it appears to be one of the most beautiful trees on my place. Every branch seems to be reaching up to the light and stands almost like a wax candle, but I never get any fruit from it. I have another tree, which was so full of fruit last year that the branches almost touched the ground. If we only get down low enough, my friends, God will use every one of us to His glory…. The holiest Christians are the humblest."[32]

When our prayers focus only on ourselves and our needs, they bear little fruit. When our prayers are focused on the Lord and *His* desires, they produce abundantly. To yield what *we* want to what *He* wants is not only the key to prayer, but the key to success in every area of our lives.

Between the humble and contrite heart and the majesty of heaven there are no barriers; the only password is prayer.

■■■

But this is the one to whom I will look, to the humble and contrite in spirit, who trembles at my word.

Isaiah 66:2 NRSV

*J*ames Gilmour, a missionary to Mongolia, was once asked to treat some wounded soldiers. Although Gilmour was not a doctor, he had some knowledge of first aid, so he felt he should help the men the best he could. He cleaned and dressed the wounds of two of the soldiers, but the third man's leg was badly broken. The missionary had no idea what to do for such an injury.

Kneeling beside the man, he humbly asked the Lord for guidance. He rose, confident that help would be supplied. No sooner had he finished his prayer than a group of beggars came up and asked Gilmour for money. His heart went out to them, and he hurriedly gave them a small gift and a few kind words.

One weary beggar remained behind as the others left. The man was little more than a *walking skeleton*. Immediately, Gilmour realized the Lord had brought him a living anatomy lesson! He asked the elderly beggar if he might examine him. Carefully tracing the femur bone with his fingers, he discovered what he needed to do to set the soldier's fractured leg![33]

When we come to God with a humble heart, admitting we don't know what to do, He will answer us and show us the way.

There are few men who dare to publish to the world the prayers they make to Almighty God.

*One of his disciples said to him,
"Lord, teach us to pray."*

Luke 11:1 NRSV

The story is told of a monk who overheard two people from the nearby village praising the virtues of a holy man. The monk felt certain that they must be talking about him. To his surprise, he discovered they were talking about a humble farmer who lived a life of virtue and profound prayer.

The monk was determined to meet this man for himself to discover what it was that had motivated such great admiration. He found the farmer selling vegetables and asked him for overnight shelter. The farmer, overjoyed to be of service, welcomed the monk into his home.

After supper, the monk suggested to his host that they pray. Almost immediately, the monk heard the sound of vulgar songs coming from a group of drunks as they passed along the road outside the farmer's home. With great annoyance the monk exclaimed, "Tell me, what kind of prayer can be made with such noise and vulgarity!" The farmer replied, "A prayer that they travel safely on their way to the kingdom of God."

The old monk marveled and returned to his monastery, aware that he had never prayed a prayer as noble as that of the humble farmer.

The key to profound prayer is to first admit that you don't know how to pray.

Just when I need Him,
He is my all, answering
when upon Him I call;
tenderly watching
lest I should fall.

■ ■ ■

And God is able to make all grace
abound toward you; that ye, always
having all sufficiency in all things,
may abound to every good work.

2 Corinthians 9:8

When Walter Wangerin was a boy, he told all of his friends that his father was the strongest man alive. Then came the day when Wally climbed to the top of the backyard cherry tree. A storm blew up suddenly and Wally was trapped. Wind ripped through the tree with such velocity that it was all Wally could do to hang onto a branch about ten feet above the ground. "Daddy!" he shouted, and instantly, his father appeared. "Jump," he yelled up to Wally. "Jump, and I'll catch you."

Wally was frozen in fear. His big, strong dad looked quite small and frail down there on the ground, two skinny arms reaching out to catch him . Wally thought, *If I jump and Dad doesn't catch me, I'll hit the ground and die!* "No!" he screamed back. At that very moment the limb Wally was clinging to cracked at the trunk. Wally surrendered. He didn't jump — he *fell* — straight into Dad's ready arms. Crying and trembling, Wally wrapped his arms and legs around his father. Dad *was* strong after all. Up to that point, it had only been a theory. Now, it was a reality; it was *experience*.[34]

Prayer is about surrendering our will to His, yielding our strength to His, giving up our desires to take on His, and surrendering when He asks us to jump into His waiting arms.

Every good and holy desire, though it lack the form, hath in itself the substance and force of a prayer with God, who regardeth the very moanings, groans, and sighings of the heart.

...for out of the abundance of the heart the mouth speaketh.

Matthew 12:34

$\mathcal{I}$n recent years, nearly every community in the United States has been equipped with a 911 emergency phone system. The newest versions of this system are state of the art. All a person has to do is dial those three numbers and he is instantly connected to a dispatcher.

The dispatcher's computer screen identifies the number from which the call is being made, the address, and the name by which the telephone number is listed. The system is simultaneously connected to the police department, fire department, and paramedics. A person using the 911 system doesn't even need to utter a word in order for help to be activated and dispatched to the scene.

The Lord has long had His own 911 system — a system more foolproof, failproof, and faithful than anything man can hope to design. When we "dial" 911 prayers, we are sometimes hysterical, or we don't know the right words to convey the deep need we feel. But God hears. He already knows our name and all about our circumstances. He knows the precise *answer* to our need even before we voice it. His help is on the way the very moment we turn to Him.[35]

Prayer always gets through to God no matter where a person might be.

From the depths...I called for help, and you listened to my cry.

Jonah 2:2 NIV

*A*fter two failed attempts at landing, a balloonist panicked. Frantically, he searched for a third spot to attempt a touchdown, but all he could see for miles was thick woods. He had only half of one tank of fuel left. Nevertheless, he felt his only option was to hit the burners and try to find a clearing. Nearly paralyzed with fear, he cried out to God, "Help me. Take control of this situation. Lord, find me a safe place to land!" With that prayer, a feeling of calm came over him. His fingers unclenched and he felt a wave of peace.

Even so, the landscape below sped by and he had no idea where his ground crew might be. Then he spotted a small clearing directly ahead — and in it, two of the biggest bulls he had ever seen. "Lord, I trusted You to find me a safe place to land, and I trust You completely with those bulls!" He held on tightly as the basket hit the ground roughly, tipped over, and was dragged along the ground for about fifty yards.

To his amazement, the bulls seemed oblivious to all the commotion. Almost instantly, his ground crew came racing toward him. One of them said, "You got caught in some nasty wind shear. It's a miracle you kept control." The balloonist knew the true miracle. *The true miracle was that he had given up control.*[36]

God may not always answer our prayers the way we think they ought to be answered. When we give up all control, and simply trust Him, He will handle any obstacle that gets in our way.

If our heart is far from God, the words of prayer are in vain.

■ ■ ■

If our consciences are clear,
we can come to the Lord with
perfect assurance and trust.

1 John 3:21 TLB

*I*n *My Utmost for His Highest*, Oswald Chambers wrote, "Conscience is that ability within me that attaches itself to the highest standard I know, and then continually reminds me of what the standard demands that I do. It is the eye of the soul which looks out either toward God or toward what we regard as the highest standard. This explains why conscience is different in different people. If I am in the habit of continually holding God's standard in front of me, my conscience will always direct me to God's perfect law and indicate what I should do. The question is, will I obey?...

"God always instructs us down to the last detail.... He does not speak with a voice like thunder — His voice is so gentle that it is easy for us to ignore. And the only thing that keeps our conscience sensitive to Him is the habit of being open to God on the inside. When you begin to debate, stop immediately. Don't ask, 'Why can't I do this?' You are on the wrong track. There is no debating possible once your conscience speaks. Whatever it is — drop it, and see that you keep your inner vision clear."[37]

Prayer unites
the soul to God.

■ ■ ■

O My Father, if it is possible,
let this cup pass from Me; nevertheless,
not as I will, but as You will.

Matthew 26:39 NKJV

𝒥n the Middle Ages, an elaborate ceremony surrounded the conferring of knighthood. After certain rites had been performed, the candidate was conducted into his lord's chapel, where he was told to keep a vigil until sunrise. He was to pass the night by "bestowing himself in visions and prayer."

This ritual was captured by artist John Pettie, in a painting he entitled "The Vigil." In it, a young armor-clad knight is seen kneeling before an altar. The light of dawn illuminates the dim aisles of the chapel behind him, but the knight doesn't seem to notice that his vigil is over. His noble but weary young face is still turned to the altar. His eyes have the look of one who has meditated at length on divine and holy things. His helmet and armor are laid on the steps leading to the altar, but he holds his sword in front of him. Its silhouette makes the form of a cross.[38]

What is it that compels you to keep a prayer vigil? Are you holding the cross before you as you pray?

It is the cross that speaks to us of complete surrender to God's will, and compels us to follow Christ wherever He leads. It is the cross that unites us to God.

Prayer is not overcoming God's reluctance; it is laying hold of His highest willingness.

Beloved, I wish above all things that thou mayest prosper and be in health, even as thy soul prospereth.

3 John 2

$\mathscr{A}$ poor young artist called her aunt one day to let her know that she was leaving on a trip to try to sell her wood carvings of sea birds to the owner of the gift shop at a fashionable resort. She asked her aunt to pray that her venture would be successful. Her aunt assured her that she would pray for the largest order she had ever received!

That evening, the young artist called her aunt back. With great exuberance she told her aunt what had happened. Not only had the gift-shop owner purchased all of her carvings, but the owner of a chain of gift shops had ordered as many carvings as she could make! She was filled with wonder at how abundantly God had answered prayer. "Now," she said to her aunt, "pray that I can fill his order!"

Her aunt wisely replied, "The Lord doesn't open a door for us unless He expects us to walk through it successfully. When you pray for rain, don't be surprised when you get a cloudburst!"[39]

Are you praying for God to meet a need in your life today? Are you expecting a bare-minimum, meager-but-satisfactory answer? Or, are you expecting an abundant, more-than-enough supply? Our God is a generous Giver!

Praying without faith
is like trying to cut
with a blunt knife —
much labour expended
to little purpose.

■ ■ ■

*But ask in faith, never doubting, for
the one who doubts is like a wave of the
sea, driven and tossed by the wind.*

James 1:6 NRSV

In Beyond Ourselves, author Catherine Marshall tells how one of her first lessons in living by faith came when she faced a problem financing her college education. She and her family lived in a small town in West Virginia that had undergone severe financial struggles in the aftermath of the 1929 stock-market crash. The two railroad shops, which were the only industry in town, were nearly shut down. Her father, a minister, suffered along with everyone else.

Even with the promise of a small work scholarship and $125 she had saved, Catherine was several hundred dollars short of what she needed to attend college.

One night her mother came to her room and found her sobbing. Her dreams of college seemed dashed. Her mother said, "You and I are going to pray about this." They went to the guest room so they wouldn't be disturbed. Her mother said, "Whenever we ask God for something that is His will, He hears us. If He hears us, then He grants the request we have made. So you and I can rest on that promise." The answer came quickly. Catherine's mother was offered a job writing the history of their county. History had long been one of her mother's loves and she made enough in this job to pay for Catherine's college expenses with a little to spare. Catherine concluded, "I learned that we must have faith *before* the fact, not after."[40]

Prayer changes
everything:
It changes the one
who prays, and it
changes the one
prayed for.

*And the Lord turned the captivity
of Job, when he prayed for his friends.*
Job 42:10

$\mathcal{A}$ young woman lay in a hospital, far from home and family, drifting in and out of consciousness. Several times she became aware of a woman's voice praying for her salvation, as well as for her physical healing. At one point, a physician described her condition as critical, warning those present in the room that she might not survive. She heard all of this as if she were in a stupor, unable to respond. Then she heard a second voice, one that spoke in faith: "Doctor, I respect what you say, but I cannot accept it. I've been praying and I believe she will not only recover, but she will walk out of here and live for God."

Before long, the young woman did walk out of that hospital and return to work. It was then she learned that it had been her boss's wife (whom she had met only twice) who had stood in the gap, interceding for her at her hospital bed. When she attempted to thank this woman for her prayers, she replied, "Don't thank me, thank God. Others have prayed for me. Their prayers changed my life. I believe God has great plans for you."

It was five more years before she gave her life to Christ, but all the while, she never forgot how a faithful woman of God had believed He would answer prayer.[41]

Have someone's prayers for you brought a change in your life? Be assured, your prayers for others will too!

Prayer does not change God, but changes him who prays.

For I am the Lord, I do not change.

Malachi 3:6 AMP

*T*wo friends, who were in love with men who had deep-seated problems, decided to meet weekly to fast and pray. Over the weeks and months that followed, they prayed for every possible "angle" related to the difficulties their loved ones were experiencing — from physiology to prenatal memories, from early-childhood experiences to spiritual conversion, from lack of ability to communicate to physical healing from addictions. One of the women said, "We were praying for a *total* healing in their lives. Looking back, I realize we were also asking God to remake them into the men *we* thought they should be, and which we genuinely thought God wanted them to be."

After nearly a year, both of the women thought they had prayed all they could and must now trust God. "Nothing happened to improve our relationships," one of the women said. "Both men went their own way and we know of no change in their attitudes or behavior. What *did* happen was that my friend and I were changed. *We* were the ones who were healed of broken hearts and shattered dreams. *We* were the ones who had our faith renewed and our hope restored. God surely will work in their lives, but the real miracle happened in us!"

When we pray for change in others, we may not get what we expect. Often, we are changed, as a result of spending time with God and caring for others enough to spend time praying on their behalf.

The deepest wishes of the heart find expression in secret prayer.

■ ■ ■

*For there is not a word
on my tongue, but, lo, O Lord,
thou knowest it altogether.*

Psalm 139:4

John Vianney, who is considered a saint, has written beautifully about the heart's cry of prayer, and the need to pray with a pure heart:

"Prayer is a fragrant dew, but we must pray with a pure heart to feel this dew. There flows from prayer a delicious sweetness, like the juice of very ripe grapes. Troubles melt away before a fervent prayer like snow before the sun. To approach God one should go straight to him, like a ball from a cannon. Prayer disengages our soul from matter; it raises it on high, like the fire that inflates a balloon. The more we pray, the more we wish to pray. Like a fish which at first swims on the surface of the water, and afterwards plunges down and is always going deeper, the soul plunges, dives, and loses itself in the sweetness of conversing with God. Prayer is the holy water that by its flow makes the plants of our good desires grow green and flourish, that cleanses our souls of their imperfections, and that quenches the thirst of passion in our hearts."[42]

It is out of the deepest recesses of the heart that our most passionate prayers arise. It is about our unspoken dreams and secret desires that we need to pray most. It is in this area of our soul that prayer does its most powerful work.

Prayer — secret, fervent, believing prayer — lies at the root of all personal godliness.

*Epaphras who is one of you,
a servant of Christ, saluteth you,
always labouring fervently for you
in prayers, that ye may stand perfect
and complete in all the will of God.*

Colossians 4:12

*A*n English minister, Leslie Stokes, once told the following parable:

Once upon a time there was a tree — a lovely tree, shapely, strong, and stately. However, appearances cannot always be trusted. Inwardly, the tree knew that its massive strength was beginning to wane. When the wind was strong it felt itself shaking ominously. It heard suspicious creaks and groans in its wood. The tree attempted to compensate for this weakness by growing another branch or two. It then looked stronger and safer than ever.

When the next gale blew, however, there was a terrific snapping of roots, and but for the support of a friendly neighboring tree, the stately tree would have crashed to the ground.

Over time, the tree recovered from its shock and began to re-anchor its roots, albeit its shape had been altered and it now leaned slightly. It looked at its neighbor with curiosity, wondering how it had withstood the storm. The tree asked, "How is it that you not only stood your ground but were able to help me?"

The neighboring tree replied, "That's easy to answer. When you were busy growing new branches, I was growing deeper roots."[43]

Prayer causes our roots to grow, strengthening us, so that our branches are able to support others and produce fruit.

Prayer is a sincere, sensible, affectionate pouring out of the soul to God.

Likewise the Spirit also helps in our weaknesses. For we do not know what we should pray for as we ought....
Romans 8:26 NKJV

A minister once attended a conference at which a number of notable Christian leaders were present. The conversation was intense, and the minister found it almost impossible to keep up with the theological and philosophical issues being discussed. At lunch time, several of the ministers gathered at a nearby restaurant, and a seminary professor was asked to pray before the meal. The minister thought to himself as he bowed his head, *This is going to sound like theology class.*

To the minister's great surprise, the professor prayed, "Father, I love being alive today. And I love sitting down with my brothers, eating good food and talking about kingdom business. I know You're at this table and I'm glad. I want to tell You in front of these brothers that I love You, and I'll do anything for You that You ask me to do." His simple prayer came from his heart, not his intellect.

So often in prayer we attempt to *sound* like theologians — using "thee" and "thou" language and lofty phrases, as if we are attempting to impress God with our understanding. The fact is, God knows what we *are not* as well as He knows what we *are*. While He is not impressed with our knowledge and understanding, He desires to impress upon us, with His indelible stamp of grace, His identity and righteousness.[44]

Prayer is not eloquence, but earnestness.

*The Lord looks down from heaven...
to see if there are any who
understand, who seek God.*

Psalm 14:2 NKJV

$\mathcal{M}$atthew Huffman, the son of missionaries in Salvador, Brazil, awoke one morning complaining of a fever. As his temperature soared, he began to lose his eyesight. His mother and father put him in the car and raced to the nearest hospital. As they drove, the boy lay in his mother's lap, listless. Then suddenly, he put one hand into the air. His mother took it gently and pulled it down to his body. He extended it again. Again, she pulled it down. A third time, he reached into the air. Confused at this unusual behavior, she asked her son, "What are you reaching for?" He answered, "I'm reaching for Jesus' hand."

With those words, Matthew closed his eyes and slid into a coma from which he never awakened. He died two days later, a victim of bacterial meningitis.

Matthew did not have a long life, but he learned the most important lesson a person can learn before he or she dies: He learned whom to reach for in the hour of death.

Matthew's upstretched hand was more eloquent than any prayer he might have made. It said in action what words could never fully convey.[45]

Are you reaching up to God today with all that you are? Not only must we reach for God at our time of death, but also for the strength to live.

Prayer is essentially man standing before his God in wonder, awe, and humility; man, made in the image of God, responding to his maker.

■ ■ ■

And God created man in His own image, in the image of God He created him.

Genesis 1:27 NASB

*D*r. George Washington Carver had this to say about prayer, "My prayers seem to be more of an attitude than anything else. I indulge in no lip service, but ask the great God silently, daily, and often many times a day, to permit me to speak to Him. I ask Him to give me wisdom, understanding, and bodily strength to do His will. Hence, I am asking and receiving all the time."

One of the most magnificent truths about God is that He meets us in every moment of prayer with the fullness of His being. He reveals Himself to us as I AM, ever-present and available. He brings the fullness of who He is to each moment of our lives. He brings not just a part of Himself, but all of Himself — His majesty, power, wisdom, and love.

Our best and highest response to such marvelous access to the fullness of the holy, omnipotent, infinite King of the universe must surely be one of awe. It matters very little what we *say*. Just to be in His presence, and to simultaneously be aware of His presence, is to be put into a position of humility, need, and provision.

Rousseau once noted, "To write a good love letter, you will begin without knowing what you are going to say, and end without knowing what you have said." The same is true for prayer. To be in God's presence and to have a relationship with Him is all that matters.[46]

Prayer is the breath of the soul, the organ by which we receive Christ into our parched and withered hearts.

Blessed is the man who listens to me,
watching daily at my gates,
waiting at the posts of my doors.
For whoever finds me finds life,
and obtains favor from the Lord.

Proverbs 8:34,35 NKJV

*I*n the midst of her intense grief, Betty found it very difficult to pray. She felt herself drowning in a sea of turbulent emotions and hardly knew her own name, much less what to request from God.

One afternoon, a friend of Betty's came by and soon, Betty was pouring out to her all of her hurts, fears, and struggles. She admitted she was angry with God, and disappointed that her prayers for her husband's healing weren't answered. She admitted she was having difficulty believing for anything — present or future. Finally, as the well of her emotions began to run dry, Betty's friend said quietly, "I have only one word of advice to give you. Let's talk to Christ."

Betty's friend put her arms around her and prayed a simple heartfelt prayer, claiming Christ's promise to heal her broken heart and restore her soul. After she had finished, she said, "Christ is with you. He is in you. And where He is, because of Who He is, He heals."

No matter what you may be going through today, your best recourse is to invite Jesus Christ to manifest Himself in you and through you. He knows the answer — He *is* the answer. He gives you Himself, and in Him is all the power, strength, encouragement, love, and comfort you need.

Don't bother to give God instructions; just report for duty.

Apply your heart to instruction, and your ears to words of knowledge.

Proverbs 23:12 NKJV

𝓜any of us show up for prayer times with a long list of things we want God to do for us. We also often include instructions about *how* we want Him to accomplish these things.

Ruby Johnson has referred to such prayers as "pea soup prayers." She has said, "Curt taught us about 'pea soup prayers.' When he was in grade school, he walked home for lunch every day. As he walked, he would pray something like, 'Please Lord, don't let Mom fix pea soup today.'

"Why did he pray like that? The answer is probably obvious: he hated pea soup. No matter how hungry he was, a bowl of that 'green goop' just didn't appeal to him at all. He knew it was nutritious and good for him, but that did not change his view in the least. Nutritious or not, he wanted no part of pea soup."

According to Johnson, a pea-soup prayer is when, "instead of allowing Him to intervene and solve the problem in His own way...we tell Him how to provide the solution.... [Curt] recognized God's superior abilities, but on the other hand he played the superior role by advising God. Absurd, isn't it?"[47]

In praying for God's will to be done, we must first dismiss our own will from the room.

God's giving is inseparably connected with our asking.

You do not have,
because you do not ask.

James 4:2 NRSV

𝓜any years ago, just after World War I, there was a grocer who tried to weigh a prayer. During the week before Christmas a woman came into his store and asked for food to make a Christmas dinner for her children. He asked her how much she had to spend. She answered, "My husband was killed in the war. I have nothing to offer but a prayer."

The grocer said gruffly, "Write it down," and went about his business. To his surprise, the woman took a slip of paper out of her purse and handed it to him. "I did that during the night while I was watching over my sick baby," she said. The grocer took the paper and callously placed it on the weight side of his old-fashioned scales. He said, "I'll give you the weight of food equal to the weight of this prayer."

To his great astonishment, when he put a loaf of bread on the other side of the scale it didn't budge. Startled, he added a brick of cheese, and then a turkey, but it still didn't move. Finally, he had loaded so much food on the scale it couldn't hold any more. He handed the woman a bag and said, "You'll have to sack it all yourself," then turned away. It was only after the woman left, tears of joy streaming down her face, that he discovered his scale had broken at the precise moment he placed her prayer on it. For the first time, he looked down to read what the woman had written: "Please, Lord, give us this day our daily bread." (Matthew 6:11.)[48]

Prayer is a cry of hope.

Put your hope in God, for I will yet praise him, my Savior and my God.

Psalm 42:5 NIV

Carolyn, a preacher's wife, had just found evidence that her daughter was involved in activities that Carolyn knew were not only sinful, but potentially deadly. Because of her position, however, Carolyn felt that to tell anyone this family secret might expose her husband and his ministry to ridicule or shame. To keep the secret was painful — she needed a friend. In near desperation, she cried out to God, "I've got to talk to *someone!* Can't You send me somebody I can trust?"

Almost before she had finished praying, the doorbell rang. When she opened the door, there stood another preacher's wife. She was new to the city and had come to make her acquaintance. Almost immediately the women developed a rapport as they discussed their lives, their many moves, and the difficulties of raising children.

Carolyn discovered her newfound friend had also gone through the struggle of raising a rebellious teenager. She poured out her problem to her new friend, who offered, "Would you mind if I prayed for you before I go?" Within minutes, Carolyn felt a profound peace fill her heart. She realized God had sent her help the very *minute* she needed it. In that, she felt confident she could trust Him to begin a healing in her daughter's heart, and in her own heart, just as quickly![49]

In prayer it is better to
have a heart without
words, than words
without a heart.

*And when you pray, you shall not
be like the hypocrites. For they love
to pray standing in the synagogues
and on the corners of the streets, that
they may be seen by men. Assuredly,
I say to you, they have their reward.*

Matthew 6:5 NKJV

*A*lthough their denominations and doctrinal positions may disagree, nearly all notable Christian leaders seem to agree on this one point: God works within us and speaks to us in stillness. God looks on the heart, and a pure heart attuned to Him is of far more value to Him than many words. Here is what some have said:

"God wants quiet; He works in silence; He needs serenity to act, and time to calm us down. Like present-day servants, He insists on one point: that we treat Him with consideration, that we take time and trouble to think of Him." — Louis Evely in *Teach Us How To Pray*[50]

"There's no use slamming on the brakes and stopping our car on a dime if the motor inside keeps whirling at top speed." — Trappist monk

"Some of the best times in prayer are wordless times. I stop speaking, close my eyes, and meditate upon what I have been reading or upon what I have been saying, and I listen inside of myself." — Charles R. Swindoll in *Three Steps Forward, Two Steps Back*[51]

"We cannot put ourselves directly in the presence of God if we do not practice internal and external silence." — Mother Teresa in *Life in the Spirit*[52]

In prayer, silence is not the absence of sound. It is the sound of being fully submitted to hear God's voice.

To look around
is to be distressed.
To look within
is to be depressed.
To look up
is to be blessed.

■ ■ ■

...looking unto Jesus...who endured such hostility from sinners against Himself, lest you become weary and discouraged in your souls.

Hebrews 12:2,3 NKJV

After two long days of lying on the ocean floor in their disabled submarine, the sub's crew members received orders from their commanding officer to sing the following hymn:

Abide with me! Fast falls the eventide.
The darkness deepens — Lord, with me abide!
When other helpers fail and comforts flee,
Help of the helpless, oh, abide with me!

After the hymn had been sung, the commander explained to his men that the hymn was his prayer for them, and that he hoped it would hold the same meaning for them as it did for him. He then explained that based upon the best information he had, they did not have long to live. There was little to no hope of outside aid, because any searchers who may be on the surface did not know the vessel's position.

Sedatives were distributed to the men to quiet their nerves. One sailor, overcome at the commander's news, fainted. As he swooned, he fell against a piece of equipment, setting in motion the surfacing mechanism that had been jammed! The submarine rose to the surface safely and soon made port.[53]

When we hit bottom in life, prayer is our best resort, for only God knows how to constrain the forces that are keeping His blessings from reaching us!

Praying is letting one's own heart become the place where the tears of God and the tears of God's children can merge and become tears of hope.

Blessed are those who mourn, for they shall be comforted.

Matthew 5:4 NASB

*A*my Carmichael landed in India in 1897. As a missionary, she devoted her first few years there to itinerant evangelism. As she traveled and became acquainted with the people, to her horror she discovered that there was "secret traffic" in the area: little girls were being sold or given for temple prostitution.

With anguished tears, Amy diligently prayed that God would enable her to find a way to rescue some of these girls. No one had ever known such a girl to escape. Nonetheless, Amy continued to pray, believing she was praying the will of Heaven and that God would answer her heart's cry.

Several years passed, but then suddenly her prayer was answered. A little girl escaped and came — led by an angel, Amy believed — straight to her. That first escape opened the way for other girls to be rescued.

Shortly thereafter, Amy discovered that little boys were being used for homosexual purposes by drama societies connected with Hindu temple worship. She prayed for the boys as she had for the girls, with many tears and much faith. Within a few years, Amy had become *Amma* ("Mother") to a rapidly growing Indian family that eventually numbered 900 children![54]

When prayer moves you to tears, your faith will no doubt move you to action.

Human life is a constant want, and ought to be a constant prayer.

Rejoice always, pray without ceasing, in everything give thanks; for this is the will of God in Christ Jesus for you.

1 Thessalonians 5:16-18 NKJV

$\mathcal{A}$fter attending an early church service one Sunday morning, Bill stopped at a cafe for breakfast. The cafe was empty, except for two elderly men sitting at the counter. They were obviously regulars, because one of the men became quite upset that his usual waiter was not on duty that morning. When the waitress started to pour him a cup of coffee, he cried, "No, no! I never drink coffee. I drink hot chocolate. Where is my waiter? What are you doing here? He always knows what I want for breakfast."

On the verge of tears, the woman retreated to the kitchen area. Bill, who had overheard their conversation thought, *I've already had my morning devotionals and said my prayers at church, but perhaps it's time to pray again.* He said in a whisper, "God, please make this man's day a little easier for him. Let him find a soft spot in his heart for this hard-working waitress." A short while later, the young woman returned to bring food to the two men and the one who had been so rude to her said tenderly, "I'm sorry, my dear. I don't know what came over me. What I said was very rude of me. I hope I didn't hurt your feelings."[55]

Any time is a good time to pray. Any circumstance is a great opportunity! As Francis de Sales once said, "Give Him your whole soul a thousand times in the day."[56]

When we pray we commit ourselves to what it is we really value in the world.

■ ■ ■

But strive first for the kingdom of God and his righteousness, and all these things will be given to you as well.

Matthew 6:33 NRSV

*O*ne day a woman couldn't help but notice that her young nephew was feeling a bit antsy. The boy was generally an even-tempered, attentive child, but on this particular day he could not seem to keep his mind on the chore she had assigned him. Finally, with genuine concern, she asked, "Is something wrong?" He nodded. "Why don't you tell me about it?" she asked.

"Auntie," He said, "I've lost my favorite marble. It's a cat eye and it took me forever to get it in the first place. Now it's gone." "Why don't we pray about it?" she asked.

Together, they knelt by a nearby chair. Immediately after their prayer, the boy seemed to be in a calmer mood and his chore was finished quickly.

The next day, almost afraid to mention it lest her nephew still be missing his favorite marble, the aunt asked cautiously, "Dear, did you find your missing treasure?"

"No," the boy replied cheerfully, "But God has made me not want to."[57]

When we pray, we may find that we don't always get what we thought we wanted. But if we pray sincerely with an open heart, we sometimes find that our heart's desires change to conform to what God truly desires to give us.

Daily prayers lessen daily cares.

Let, I pray thee, thy merciful kindness be for my comfort, according to thy word unto thy servant.

Psalm 119:76

$\mathcal{I}$t was almost planting season and a farmer found himself without any money to buy seed. He had prepared his fields for planting, anticipating that the bank would lend him money for seed, as they had for several years. This year, however, the bank had changed its policy — no more seed money.

The farmer didn't know what to do, except to talk to God about the problem during his morning devotional time. As he prayed, the idea came to him, *Perhaps the co-op will advance me the seed*. He knew the co-op rule: credit for fertilizer, chemicals, and fuel — but seed had to be paid for in cash. Even so, he decided to go talk to the co-op manager. Upon arriving at the co-op office, the secretary greeted him warmly and handed him an envelope as she ushered him into the manager's office. "What's this?" he asked. The manager replied, "Your payment for last year's crop."

"I didn't think it was due for several months," the farmer said as he opened the envelope. The manager smiled and said, "This year we decided to do it earlier."

"Thank you!" the farmer blurted out as he saw the amount of the check — $10,000 *more* than he needed. "Now what did you want to talk to me about this morning?" the manager asked. "Not a thing," the farmer replied thinking, *Talking to God has already taken care of it.*[58]

Make every matter of care a matter of prayer.

Casting all your care upon him; for he careth for you.

1 Peter 5:7

In He Still Moves Stones, Max Lucado writes: "What matters to you matters to God. You probably think that's true when it comes to the big stuff. When it comes to the major-league difficulties like death, disease, sin, and disaster — you know that God cares. But what about the smaller things? What about grouchy bosses or flat tires or lost dogs? What about broken dishes, late flights, toothaches, or a crashed hard disk? Do these matter to God?

"I mean, He's got a universe to run. He's got the planets to keep balanced and presidents and kings to watch over. He's got wars to worry with and famines to fix. Who am I to tell Him about my ingrown toenail? I'm glad you asked. Let me tell you who you are...you are God's child.... As a result, if something is important to you, it's important to God."[59]

In labeling something as a "big" problem, we are implying that it will take God more effort to resolve it. To say something is a "little" problem implies less effort. The fact is, there are no degrees of difficulty to One who is omnipotent. God's all-powerful, and therefore, all-capable. He knows all the solutions, even as He knows all the problems. No problem, big or small, is beyond His love, concern, and ability.

Living a life without prayer is like building a house without nails.

Unless the Lord builds the house, its builders labor in vain.

Psalm 127:1 NIV

$\mathcal{I}$n 1787, the Constitutional Convention was on the brink of failure over the issue of whether small states should have the same representation as the larger states. The situation seemed hopeless, and many of the delegates were making plans to return home, when 81-year-old Benjamin Franklin offered a suggestion. He was convinced that Scripture is right when it says, "Except the Lord build the house, they labour in vain that build it" (Psalm 127:1). He rose to address the delegates:

> Gentlemen, I have lived a long time and am convinced that God governs in the affairs of men. If a sparrow cannot fall to the ground without His notice, is it probable that an empire can rise without His aid? I move that prayer imploring the assistance of Heaven be held every morning before we proceed to business.

His motion carried. Every morning thereafter, the sessions opened with prayer. In a short while, a compromise was forged. It is still in effect today — a fixed representation for states in the Senate, representation according to population in the House.[60]

The best building material for constructing any solution you may need today is prayer.

Prayer is the channel of all blessings and the secret of power and life.

For everyone who asks, receives. Anyone who seeks, finds. If only you will knock, the door will open.

Matthew 7:8 TLB

*E*verywhere the minister had gone that day, he had encountered crisis. He had offered a listening ear, a consoling word, and patient understanding until he was completely drained. Arriving home late in the day, he put on his jogging shoes and headed out for a run. He hoped the exercise would restore his sense of well-being and balance.

As he put on his shoes, he reached into the pocket of his sweatshirt and pulled out a frayed devotional book he often read before his run. He felt like screaming as he read the "thought for today": *Pray for others.*

"Pray for others?" he said. "All I've done today is give to others. What about me? Who cares about my needs?"

He felt angry that God was calling him to still more giving, but eventually he yielded. In the rhythm of his feet hitting the pavement, he prayed for his neighbors and the people he had met during the day. As he turned his steps toward home, he prayed for his family.

Upon arriving home, the minister realized he was refreshed both spiritually and physically and ready to "give some more."[61]

Is there power in prayer? Most assuredly! It is God's power bestowed *to us* and *in us*, so that we might serve others.

Nothing lies beyond the reach of prayer except that which lies beyond the will of God.

There is a way that seems right to a man, but its end is the way of death.

Proverbs 14:12 NKJV

A little girl desperately wanted a new bicycle. She had been playing with a neighbor girl who had a new bicycle, and more than anything, she wanted to trade in her "baby bike" for a real "big girl" model like the one her friend rode. When she asked her parents for a new one, they both said, "Wait until your birthday."

Two weeks later, the little girl saw a picture of a bicycle in the newspaper. She stared at it in awe. The ad read, "Three speeds. Gear shifts. Light and easy to handle. Hand brakes. In many colors. The works!" She asked her parents if they might visit the store where the bike was sold and they agreed. To her delight, she found the bicycle came in hot pink! "But don't you want a bike just like your friend has?" Mom asked with a smile. "No way," the little girl replied. "I've got something better in mind!"[62]

We can very often look back with thanksgiving that God did *not* answer our prayers. His answer reflected something better that we hadn't known about, or thought to request!

Praying "thy kingdom come, thy will be done" need never be a prayer of passivity. It can be a powerful prayer of submission and faith: We want God's best, but at the same time, we recognize only He knows what that may be!

If your prayers are sincere, then you can be sure that [your] present life is exactly what God knows is best...for you!

Lord God of Israel, there is no God in heaven or on earth like You, who keep Your covenant and mercy with Your servants who walk before You with all their hearts.

2 Chronicles 6:14 NKJV

*A*dmiral Sir Thomas Williams was in command of a ship that routinely crossed the Atlantic. His course brought him in sight of Ascension Island, which was uninhabited most of the time. The island was visited only once a year for the purpose of collecting turtles.

The island was barely visible on the horizon during one crossing, when Sir Thomas felt a great urge to steer his vessel toward it. The closer he came to the island, the greater the urgency he felt. When he gave the order to head for the island, his lieutenant officer respectfully pointed out that such a course change would greatly delay them. Even so, the admiral remained intent. The inner urging, which he had come to recognize as God's Spirit inside him, was very strong.

As the ship neared the island, his crew spotted a white flag. "It must be a signal!" Williams concluded. Sure enough, as the ship neared the beach, they found sixteen men, who wrecked on the coast many days before. They were starving and had nearly given up hope of rescue.[63]

In prayer, we are called upon to yield the rudder of our soul to God, so that He might steer us toward His blessings, or to opportunities to bless others.

Much prayer, much power. Little prayer, little power.

*Show the wonder of your great love,
you who save by your right hand those
who take refuge in you from their foes.
Keep me as the apple of your eye;
hide me in the shadow of your wings.*

Psalm 17:7,8 NIV

A middle-aged man looked in the mirror one day and didn't like what he saw. His formerly lean, muscular body had become flabby. Although he had enjoyed physical exertion as a young man, he now detested exercise. Not only did he find it a waste of time, but he hated the aches and pains associated with it. He had a long track record of starting, stopping, starting, and stopping an exercise program. The result? He remained unfit.

Then one day, he picked up Kenneth Cooper's book, *Aerobics*, in which Dr. Cooper documents the importance and benefits of exercising the heart. The man read the book again several times and started jogging regularly. He didn't read the book for information or to become convinced; he was already informed and convinced. He reread the book for motivation. Eventually, exercise became its own motivation. He began to *enjoy* exercise because he liked the results![64]

We can know prayer is valuable, and be convinced it is important. But it is only when we pray in a disciplined manner that we truly become motivated to pray further. Why is this so? Because prayer empowers us. The more we feel empowered by God, the more we desire to become empowered. The net result is spiritual fitness — a greater capacity to serve others and experience abundant life.

Strength in prayer is better than length in prayer.

*I will pray with the spirit, and I will
pray with the understanding also:
I will sing with the spirit, and I will
sing with the understanding also.*

1 Corinthians 14:15

*J*oni Eareckson Tada lives such an inspirational life of ministry today, it is often difficult for others to accept the fact that in the wake of her paralyzing accident, Joni experienced nearly three years of depression and suicidal despair. She finally reached the point where she prayed, "God, if I can't die, show me how to live, please!" Prayers of desperation do not need to be lengthy.

Things didn't change for Joni overnight, but they did begin to change. Very little about her *situation* changed, but her outlook — her attitude, her mind, her perspective, her spirit — began to change and grow. She knew with an increasing assurance that God would help her learn how to do what seemed to be impossible: handle life in a wheelchair.[65]

Are you facing a seemingly impossible situation today? Do you feel as if any option you have is one you don't like, and which can't bring you any sense of peace or reward? Perhaps it's time to pray with strength: "God, show me how to live in the midst of this situation." Accepting God's help in coping with the despair and hopelessness of a situation is very often the first step God uses in preparing us to live a new way — a way that is far beyond mere coping. His way is always one of true fulfillment and joy.

Prayer is invading the impossible.

"Sun, stand still over Gibeon; and Moon, in the Valley of Aijalon." So the sun stood still, and the moon stopped.

Joshua 10:12,13 NKJV

$\mathcal{D}$uring World War II, a missionary family lived near a place where the Japanese tortured and killed their captives. The family was often awakened by the screams of the tormented. Twice, the missionary was taken captive and released unharmed. The third time the officer said to the missionary's wife, "He has been returned to you two times — don't think he will be spared a third time. This time he dies."

After she had put her five children to bed, the wife began a prayer vigil. At four o'clock, she awoke her family to join her, saying, "The burden has become so heavy I cannot bear it alone." A short while later, they heard footsteps — ones she recognized as those of her husband!

Safely inside their home, he told her what had happened. He had been the last in a row of ten men. A Japanese soldier had gone down the row, slashing off the head of each man with a sword. Just as he raised his sword to kill the missionary, the officer shouted, "Stop!" Then he roared to the missionary, "Go home. Quick, get out of here!" He pushed the missionary past the guard and toward the gate. "I looked at my watch," the missionary said. "It was 4 AM."[66]

Nothing impacts the impossible more than prayer.

Those who quietly,
through prayer,
used God's power,
were the ones who
made the world
move forward.

*Make progress, rise like an edifice
higher and higher —
praying in the Holy Spirit.*

Jude 20 AMP

$\mathcal{D}$r. A. B. Simpson, a New York preacher, was plagued by poor health. Two nervous breakdowns and a heart condition led a well-known New York physician to tell him — at the age of thirty-eight — that he would never live to be forty. The physician's diagnosis was no surprise to Simpson. Preaching was agonizing for him; even climbing a slight elevation left him breathless.

In desperation, Simpson went to his Bible to find out what Jesus had to say about disease. He became convinced that Jesus wanted to heal him. One Friday afternoon shortly after Simpson came to this conclusion, he went for a walk in the country. Coming to a pine woods, he sat down on a log to rest and pray. He asked Christ to become his physical life until his life's work was accomplished. (Galatians 2:20.) He later said, "Every fiber in me was tingling with the sense of God's presence."

Days later, Simpson climbed a 3,000-foot mountain. He said, "When I reached the top, the world of weakness and fear was lying at my feet. From that time on I literally had a new heart." He went on to preach 3,000 sermons in the next three years, holding as many as twenty meetings a week. He amassed an amazing volume of work before he died — at the age of 76.[67]

Prayer brings [God] down to earth, and links His power with our efforts.

Thy kingdom come. Thy will be done, on earth as it is in heaven.

Matthew 6:10 NASB

A number of years ago, Pat Robertson was praying and fasting when he heard the Lord ask him, "What do I desire for man?" Startled, Robertson replied, "I don't know, Lord. You know." He was impressed to turn to the opening chapter of the Bible, where his eyes locked on the phrase, "And God said, Let us make man in our image, after our likeness: and let them have dominion."

Suddenly, he felt he knew the Lord's purpose for the life of every person — to have dominion over all things on the earth in order to bring the kingdom of God into reality. *Out of heaven...to the earth!* That was God's plan!

In his book *The Secret Kingdom*, Robertson explains: "God gives man the authority to govern all that is willing to be governed" and "He grants man authority over the untamed and the rebellious.... Implicit in the grant was a requirement that man order the planet according to God's will and for God's purposes. This was a grant of freedom, not of license."[68]

We are free today to pray anything we desire to pray. However, we are wise to pray those things which we know are according to God's will and His plan — those things which are in Heaven, which God desires to see on the earth. As we pray in that way, we can expect to see our prayers fully answered.

The sweetest lesson I have learned in God's school is to let the Lord choose for me.

■ ■ ■

For your Father knows the things you have need of before you ask Him.

Matthew 6:8 NIV

College football star Mike Rohrbach, of the University of Washington, once made three trips into the end zone in a big game against Stanford University. At the close of the game, he and about a dozen other players, from both teams, knelt in the end zone. Thousands of fans wondered what that post-game huddle was all about. So did the sportscasters. Rohrbach, a member of the Fellowship of Christian Athletes, was happy to tell them that the players had "thanked the Lord that we got a chance to compete and see each other as friends." Win or lose, they knew that the greater value of the game lay in the relationships they might develop with each other, and with God.

The same spirit of prayer invaded the Washington Redskins locker room after they were defeated in a Super Bowl by the Miami Dolphins. After the team prayed together, one of the players, who had fumbled four times, reminded his fellow team members that the real success of any person or team lay not in the way they handled a victory, but in the way they handled defeat. Any theology must survive tragedy and loss, or it is not good theology.[69]

Whether we win or lose, the Lord remains the same. That's the perspective we must always have when we pray. God does not promise us success. He promises us His presence *in all things* and His power to *face all things*.

Unanswered yet!
Nay do not say
UNGRANTED;
perhaps your part
is not yet fully done.

Moses answered and said,
But, behold, they will not believe
me...And the Lord said unto him,
What is that in thine hand?
And he said, A rod.

Exodus 4:1,2

A woman minister received a call from a friend she had not seen in two years. The friend said, "My husband is leaving me for another woman. I need for you to pray with me." The minister said, "Come quickly."

When her friend arrived, the minister could not help but notice that her friend was carelessly dressed, had become overweight, and had not combed her hair or put on makeup. As they began to converse, the friend admitted to being an uninteresting, nagging wife and a sloppy housekeeper. The minister quickly concluded to herself, *My friend has grown to hate herself!*

When her friend paused to ask for her advice, the minister said only, "Will you join me in a song?" Surprised, her friend agreed. The minister began to sing, "Jesus loves me, this I know." Her friend joined in, tears flooding her eyes. "If Jesus loves me, I must love myself, too," she concluded.

Amazing changes followed. Because she felt loved and lovable, this woman was transformed into the confident woman she once had been. In the process, she recaptured her husband's heart.

We can never accept God's love beyond the degree to which we are willing to love ourselves. We rarely receive more than we are willing to believe God has for us. Our part is to believe, to receive, and to give.

Prayer moves the hand that moves the world.

The things which are impossible with men are possible with God.

Luke 18:27

$\mathcal{B}$illy Graham had planned a meeting in Germany in 1992, but when the Berlin Wall came down in 1989, his plans changed. On March 10, 1990, Graham spoke at the Platz der Republik, the great open area in front of the Reichstag, the historic site where Nazis once paraded by torchlight, preaching their doctrine of ethnic bitterness and hatred. In sharp contrast, Graham spoke of the good news of God's forgiveness and love. Just a few yards away, workers with saws and torches continued to rip out the bars that had supported the wall.

Graham told the large congregation, "God has answered our prayers." Members of the press corps asked if he truly believed the dismantling of the Iron Curtain was an answer to prayer. He told them yes. Christians in the East and the West had been praying for decades for the day the wall would be demolished. He told them the prospect of liberation, reunification, and the freedom to worship God made this the happiest hour for Germany.[70]

Often, we mistakenly assume that major world events just happen. In nearly all cases, however, you will find that those headlines which mark major changes for good — and perhaps especially so, peace — have been birthed in prayer. God commands us to pray for all those in authority. Your prayers *do* make a difference in the world!

God's answers are wiser than our prayers.

■ ■ ■

The foolishness of God is wiser than men, and the weakness of God is stronger than men.

1 Corinthians 1:25 NKJV

A little girl watched with envy as her older brother and his friends worked a gumball machine outside the local hardware store. When she asked her brother for a gumball, he told her he didn't have any more quarters for the machine and she would have to use her own allowance for such treats.

When her father arrived at home that evening, the little girl approached him to make her request, "Daddy, can I have a quarter?" Feeling generous, the father pulled out his wallet and offered his daughter a crisp new twenty-dollar bill.

Not realizing what the bill was, the little girl refused the paper money. As far as she was concerned, it was useless — it wouldn't fit into the gumball machine. She said, "No, I don't want that. I want a *quarter*."[71]

Are there times when we deal with our Heavenly Father as this little girl dealt with her father? Do we sometimes ask for some small favor, refusing His offer of a blessing that is a hundred times more valuable?

God may not answer our prayers precisely as we would desire, but we can always know He has answered our prayers in the way that is best for us.

How deeply rooted
must unbelief be in
our hearts when we
are surprised to find
our prayer answered.

■ ■ ■

Lord, I believe;
help thou mine unbelief.
Mark 9:24

A woman once accepted a job in a field for which she had a college degree and past experience. She had community contacts, she enjoyed this type of work, and her family could use the extra income — the job seemed to be a perfect fit! Almost immediately, however, problems emerged. As the weeks wore on, she wore out. Being a die-hard, she held on, trying to force the job to work for her, and to be successful in the job. "God, please show me what I should do!" she prayed.

One cold winter day, her phone rang and a young woman said, "You probably don't remember me, but I was in a seminar group you taught about a year ago. Could I come talk to you today?" Although her schedule was full, she made an appointment with the young woman. She discovered that the young woman was in despair about her job, and was yearning to enter a field where she could express her strengths and gifts. The woman urged her to do what was right for her, to move away from what had kept her imprisoned, to choose excellence and quality, and to recognize that her gifts were from God.

It was only after the young woman left that the woman realized, "That advice I gave was for my benefit!"[72]

Don't be surprised today at how God answers your prayer. It may even come through something you say to help someone else.

Did not God
sometimes withhold
in mercy what we ask,
we should be ruined
at our own request.

■ ■ ■

*For My thoughts are not your
thoughts, neither are your ways
My ways, says the Lord.*

Isaiah 55:8 AMP

$\mathcal{W}$e live in a reasonably well-ordered society. When we mail a letter, it *usually* ends up where we wanted it to go. When we order an item from a catalog, it *usually* arrives in the size and color we requested. We are accustomed to getting what we ask for.

Our prayer life, however, cannot be directly tied to results we expect or demand. Worship and intercession involve the aligning of our will with God's purposes, not the aligning of His will to our desires. As Henri Nouwen once wrote: "In prayer we move away from ourselves, our worries, preoccupation, and self-gratification — and direct all that we recognize as ours to God in the simple trust that through His love all will be made new."[73]

In reflecting on her experiences as a quadriplegic, Joni Eareckson Tada has said, "For years I pleaded with God to give me hands and feet that would work. I never got what I wanted. Looking back, I can see God's wisdom in not granting my wish. From those torrid times of pleading, I've come away all the better for not having received my greatest desire. My faith is stronger. My love for Jesus is brighter. It wouldn't be the same had my wish been granted."[74]

Can you look back today and praise God that He didn't answer a particular prayer you prayed?

I have lived
to thank God that
all my prayers have
not been answered.

■ ■ ■

*As the heavens are higher
than the earth, so are My ways
higher than your ways, and
My thoughts than your thoughts.*

Isaiah 55:9 NKJV

*Y*ears ago, a devout woman earnestly prayed that her son might be called to preach. He grew up, accepted Christ as his Savior and Lord, and subsequently began to prepare for the calling to which he seemed destined. Before his training was complete, however, he concluded that he was not called to this work. He left school and began to work for a bank. He continued in that field and became a great financier. He died rich and successful.

When her son's will was read, the mother learned that he had left his vast fortune to a theological seminary in Kentucky. By his one act, many young men have been prepared to preach the Gospel.

Centuries earlier, another mother had a similar experience. Hearing that her son desired to visit Rome, she diligently prayed that he would not go. She feared the vices of the city would overwhelm him. Even so, he went. While in Rome, he was converted to Christianity. In his *Confessions*, Augustine writes that his mother's prayer was answered, not in its outward form, but in its inward heart. What she had really prayed for was that he might be saved from the ways of sin, and he was.[75]

In both cases, the prayers of these mothers were not granted, but they *were* answered. Today, trust God to respond to you in the way that's best for you — for eternity.

Good prayers never
come creeping home.
I am sure I shall receive
either what I ask,
or what I should ask.

*And we are sure of this, that he will
listen to us whenever we ask him
for anything in line with his will.
And if we really know he is listening
when we talk to him and make
our requests, then we can be sure
that he will answer us.*

1 John 5:14,15 TLB

While teaching a Bible class, a woman lost her place in her notes as she was speaking. As she continued to speak, she tried to find it, but when she realized she was hopelessly lost in her own muddle of words, she apologized to the group and paused to search for the missing page. The pause grew agonizingly long and at last, she gave up the search and ad-libbed her way through the rest of the lesson. She couldn't remember the applications she had planned to make, forgot part of her main illustration, and knew her conclusion was weak. As she left the lectern, she was on the verge of tears, feeling like an abysmal failure.

To her great surprise, a woman came to her to say that she thought this had been the best Bible class so far. Later, another woman called to thank her for a specific word that was just what she needed to hear.

The teacher called a friend and said, "I don't understand what happened. I had prepared the best I could." Her friend laughed and said, "Do you remember what you said last week — that you were praying these women would be able to relate to you and you to them? Perhaps that's precisely what happened. They aren't perfect, either!"[76]

When necessary, God responds to our intent, not our specific requests.

Our prayer and God's mercy are like two buckets in a well; while the one ascends, the other descends.

[Jacob] dreamed that there was a ladder set up on the earth, and the top of it reached to heaven; and the angels of God were ascending and descending on it!

Genesis 28:12 AMP

*O*ne day in Lucerne, Switzerland, a man rode to the summit of Mount Pilatus in a hydraulically-powered cable car. As the car rose along the side of the mountain, he marveled at the wonders of modern engineering. A little more than halfway to the summit, he noticed a beautiful waterfall, its water pouring down the mountainside.

What a contrast! he thought. In one glance he had a comparison of the primitive power of nature and the advanced power of technology. Then it occurred to him. The waterfall was not in contrast to the cable car. Rather, it was a complement. It was the source of the hydraulic power — it was the force of that very water that was driving the cable car.[77]

So it is with prayer. The power that takes us up to God is the same power that comes from God. He is the One who:

- calls us to pray,
- enables us to pray,
- energizes our prayers with His Spirit, and
- gives us the capacity to receive His answers.

When we pray in the name of Jesus, the Lord is in our prayers as much as He is in the answers.

God not only gives us
answers to our prayers,
but with every answer
gives us something
of Himself.

*Then you will call upon me and come
and pray to me, and I will listen to
you. You will seek me and find me
when you seek me with all your heart.*
Jeremiah 29:12,13 NIV

$\mathcal{F}$anny Crosby, the noted hymn writer, said she never attempted to write a hymn without first kneeling in prayer. Given the fact that she wrote no less than 8,000 songs, she was obviously a woman of considerable prayer!

Like many creative people, Miss Crosby was often under pressure to meet deadlines. One such time came in 1869 as she tried to write lyrics for a tune composed by W. H. Doane. She couldn't seem to find the words, and then she remembered she had forgotten to pray. As she rose from her knees, she dictated — as fast as her assistant could write — the words for the famous hymn, "Jesus, Keep Me Near the Cross."

Another time, she had run short of money and needed exactly five dollars for a particular purpose. There was no time to call upon her publishers, so she simply prayed for the money. As she ended her prayer, she began to pace back and forth in her room, trying to get into the mood to write. Just at that time, an admirer called upon her. The two chatted briefly, and in parting, the woman pressed something into her hand. It was a five-dollar bill! Fanny fell to her knees in a prayer of thanksgiving, and upon rising, wrote "All the way my Saviour leads me."[78]

Jesus does not just give answers. He is The Answer.

Prayer is for the soul what nourishment is for the body.

■ ■ ■

You will keep him in perfect peace, whose mind is stayed on You.

Isaiah 26:3 NKJV

In The Power and Blessing, Jack Hayford writes, "I had gone on vacation, and I needed it! I remember how delightful it was to get to the beach...they were great days. But about the fourth day, when everything seemed to be so relaxing, out from under pressure, I found I was feeling *empty* inside. As I thought about my good *external* feeling, I wondered about the hollowness I felt inside. Then, it occurred to me.

"For four days, I hadn't read a word of Scripture; I hadn't prayed a prayer; I hadn't once sung a song of praise. It was just kind of, 'Let's get away from it all.' Without planning or saying as much, it was as though we were so involved with church, the Bible, and prayer that we didn't want to do anything especially 'godly' for awhile....

"But I was 'called back' by the inner 'hollowness' that I felt. And through that experience I learned the impracticality of trying to recover at the physical/emotional level of my life if I neglect the spiritual level."[79]

When we are weary, rest and relaxation alone will not meet our needs. As spiritually alive creatures in Christ Jesus, our true rejuvenation comes when we go to the Fountain of Life, Jesus Himself. He gives us water that satisfies our parched souls and provides energy for our minds and bodies.

There are four answers to prayer: yes, no, wait, and if.

Wait on the Lord: be of good courage, and he shall strengthen thine heart: wait, I say, on the Lord.

Psalm 27:14

In Three Steps Forward, Two Steps Back, Charles Swindoll writes: "It's awfully hard for a country that exists on frozen dinners, instant mashed potatoes, powdered orange juice, packaged cake mixes, instant-print cameras, and freeway express lanes to teach its young how to wait.

"One evening I was fussing about seeds in the grapes my wife had served for supper. After crunching into another seed, I laid down the law. 'No more grapes served in the Swindoll home unless they are seedless!' I announced with characteristic dogmatism. Later, when nobody else was around to hear her reproof, Cynthia edged up to me and quietly asked: 'Do you know why seeds in grapes bug you?' 'Sure,' I said, 'because I bite into those bitter little things and they scatter all over my mouth!' 'No.' She smiled. 'It's because you're too impatient to dig them out first. The purple grapes really taste better...but they take a little more time.'"[80]

Two answers to prayer are decisive: yes and no. One gives us something concrete to do: if. But when God answers by saying "wait," it is perhaps the most difficult for us because we are left in suspense with little to do other than trust. Often in our impatience, we attempt to create an answer of our own. If we really want God's best, however, perhaps we should give Him all the time He needs to prepare us for it!

The primary purpose
of prayer is not
to get answers,
but to deepen our
friendship with God.

■ ■ ■

Abraham believed God...
and he was called God's friend.
James 2:23 NIV

There once was a godly man in Germany, named Bengel, who was known for his intimacy with Christ. A friend of this saintly man desired to learn his secrets, so he hid himself in Bengel's room one night. He hoped to observe his friend at devotions. Within a short while, Bengel entered the room, sat down at his table, and began reading the New Testament.

Hours passed without Bengel uttering a word. He simply read page after page. Then, as the clock struck midnight he spread out his hands and said with great joy, "Dear Lord Jesus, we are on the same old terms!"

Then closing his Bible, he climbed in bed and was soon asleep.

Bengel had learned the secret of a deep relationship with Christ — listening to Him through the Scriptures, loving Him in his heart, talking to Him as a friend.

The more we spend time with our Lord, the better we get to know Him. That knowing should be our greatest goal, and joy, in prayer. As William Cowper once wrote:

What various hindrances we meet
In coming to a mercy seat!
Yet who that knows the worth of prayer
But wishes to be often there![81]

More things are wrought by prayer than the world dreams of.

The effectual fervent prayer of a righteous man availeth much.

James 5:16

Christian cardiologist Dr. Randolph Byrd had a great interest in knowing if prayer had a "scientifically measurable" impact on healing. He has said, "After much prayer, the idea of what to do came to me." Over a ten-month period, a computer assigned 393 patients in the coronary care unit at San Francisco General Hospital to one of two groups.

The first group was prayed for by home prayer groups. The second group was not remembered in prayer. The home prayer groups were from various Christian denominations. They were given only the first names of the patients and a brief description of their diagnosis and condition. They were prayed for each day.

The prayed-for patients differed from those not prayed for in these ways:

They were five times less likely to require antibiotics; they were three times less likely to develop fluid in the lungs; none required an artificial airway attached to a ventilator; and fewer died.

If the technique being studied had been a new drug or procedure, it certainly would have been heralded as a breakthrough. Even Dr. William Nolan, the author of a book denouncing faith healing, said, "It sounds like this study will stand up to scrutiny.... Maybe we doctors ought to be writing on our order sheets, 'Pray three times a day.'"[82]

It doesn't matter what the skeptics say — prayer works.

The Christian life without prayer is like computer hardware without the software.

Call to me and I will answer you and tell you great and unsearchable things you do not know.

Jeremiah 33:3 NIV

𝓜other Teresa has said, "Prayer feeds the soul — as blood is to the body, prayer is to the soul — and it brings you closer to God. It also gives you a clean and pure heart. A clean heart can see God, can speak to God, and can see the love of God in others."

This view has been echoed by Sister Kateri, who is affiliated with the Sisters of Charity (the order founded by Mother Teresa) in the Bronx, New York. She has said:

"The most important thing that a human being can do is pray, because we've been made for God and our hearts are restless until we rest with Him. And it's in prayer that we come into contact with God....

"I used to share this with the men at the prison I visited. I'd give them the example: If you had to go on a trip, what would you need? And the men would say, 'You'd need a car and you'd need gasoline.' We used to have a good time because we usually decided that the gasoline was prayer, the car was our life, the journey was to Heaven, you had to have a map, you had to know where you were going, and so on. My point really is that the gasoline of our life is prayer and without that we won't reach our destination, and we won't reach the fulfillment of our being."[83]

The answer to our prayer may be the echo of our resolve.

...for he who comes to God must believe that He is, and that He is a rewarder of those who diligently seek Him.

Hebrews 11:6 NKJV

$\mathcal{A}$ pastor once challenged some of the young people in his congregation to spend fifteen minutes every day praying for foreign missions. But he warned them, "Beware how you pray, for I warn you, this is a very costly experiment."

"Costly?" one of the youth asked in surprise.

"Yes, costly," he replied. "When Carey began to pray for the conversion of the world it cost him himself.

"Brainerd prayed for the dark-skinned savages, and after two years of blessed work, it cost him his life.

"Two students in Mr. Moody's summer school began to pray the Lord of the harvest to send forth more servants into His harvest; and, lo, it is going to cost America five thousand young men and women who have, in answer to this prayer, pledged themselves to missions.

"Be sure it is a dangerous thing to pray in earnest for this work; you will find that you cannot pray and withhold your labour, or pray and withhold your money; indeed, you will find that your very life will no longer be your own when your prayers begin to be answered."[84]

Prayer increases our compassion, and can reveal to us God's call on our life. When we pray for certain things, God's answer may be to tell us what we can do to bring the solution to pass.

Prayer is a virtue that prevaileth against all temptations.

■ ■ ■

Watch and pray, lest you enter into temptation. The spirit indeed is willing, but the flesh is weak.

Mark 14:38 NKJV

$\mathcal{M}$ike and Teri had one major thing in common: They both wanted to make their first million dollars by the age of thirty. Teri wasn't a Christian when they met, but Mike was, and after attending church with Mike and reading Christian books he gave to her, she accepted the Lord. They were married a short while later, and for the next two years lived what both called an ideal life.

Their focus on financial success, however, caused their dreams to begin unraveling. They began to drift apart, and to drift away from Jesus Christ. Eventually, they separated and divorced. A year after the divorce, Teri went to a conference and came away believing that God could restore their marriage. She began to pray earnestly for Mike.

Not long after, Mike began to recognize that God was not finished with him. He set his heart toward God, walked away from the life he had been leading, and made contact with Teri. They remarried.[85]

Can prayer keep a marriage together? Mike and Teri believe it can. And so did Rev. and Mrs. Robert Newton. They met twice a day to pray with and for each other, every day of their more than fifty years of marriage. At their jubilee wedding anniversary, Rev. Newton said, "I know not that an unkind look or an unkind word has ever passed between us."[86]

God answers prayers because His children ask.

The Lord has given me my petition which I asked of Him.

1 Samuel 1:27 NASB

*O*ne night while Chinaman Kao Er was attending a prayer meeting, his eight-year-old son and baby daughter were kidnapped. The kidnappers demanded 1,000 yuan in ransom. Mr. Er painted a large sign and posted it in front of his place of employment. It said, "I am not a wealthy man. I cannot pay 1,000 yuan ransom. I cannot pay 500 yuan. I cannot even pay 50 yuan. But I believe God. He is able to bring my children back without ransom."

The sign brought a great deal of ridicule from those who saw it. *No sane man could expect a kidnapped child to be returned alive without ransom!* Weeks passed. Finally, soldiers clashed with bandits in the China countryside and the bandits were routed. In hot pursuit of the bandits, some soldiers heard a sound coming from a ditch beside the road. They found a skeleton-like child lying there, abandoned by the bandits. It was Mr. Er's son!

After a second battle between the bandits and soldiers, the wife of the bandit chief was captured. She was nursing two babies — one of whom was Mr. Er's daughter. Both children were returned home safely. God had done the impossible — returned kidnapped children *without ransom*.[87]

God's answers to prayer are not dependent upon our ability to pray, but on His ability to answer.

When God does not
immediately respond to
the cries of His children,
it is because He wants
to accomplish some
gracious purpose
in their lives.

*...that the testing of your faith
produces patience.*

James 1:3 NKJV

A pastor's wife was accustomed to uninvited guests and was usually delighted to have them — but not when the guests were cockroaches. She was appalled when they made their appearance in her new parsonage. The very word, "cockroaches," sounded dirty to her. She immediately sought a way to get rid of them. Spraying pesticides in the house was impossible due to the physical condition of one of her children. The only solution seemed to be the use of roach traps — a safe, but slow process. It took almost a year before the house was free of the dirty insects.

During that year, the pastor's wife encountered Romans 8:28 — "We know that all things work together for good to those who love God." She laughed and said, "Well, Lord, if You say so!" She couldn't imagine what good might come of battling cockroaches month after month.

Several weeks after the disappearance of the last cockroach, she received a letter from her daughter, who had gone to Paraguay as a missionary. She wrote: "Mom, do you remember all those awful cockroaches we had? Well, we have huge, flying ones here! I'm glad I was able to get used to them at home before coming to Paraguay!"[88]

God is in the process of perfecting you. His greatest aim is to build His character in us. He always has our ultimate good in mind!

The greatest privilege God gives to you is the freedom to approach Him at any time.

■ ■ ■

Let us then approach the throne of grace with confidence, so that we may receive mercy and find grace to help us in our time of need.

Hebrews 4:16 NIV

$\mathscr{A}$ physician once went to the home of one of his patients who was dying of lung cancer. He spent time sitting at his bedside, with the man's wife and children. The dying man knew that he had little time left and he chose his words carefully, speaking to the physician in a hoarse whisper. Although he had not been a very religious person, he revealed to his doctor that recently he had begun to pray frequently.

"What do you pray for?" the physician asked.

"I don't pray for anything," the dying man responded. "How would I know what to ask for?" The physician found this surprising. Surely this dying man could think of *some* request.

"If prayer is not for asking, what is it *for*?" the physician asked.

"It isn't *for* anything," the man said after a few moments of silent thought. "It mainly reminds me I am not alone."[89]

God desires to have a relationship with each one of us — that relationship is the very reason for our creation. Relationship with God is what gives our life meaning and purpose. Relationship is what Jesus embodied, and what the Holy Spirit establishes. Relationship is *why* we pray, and why we have the privilege of praying.

Prayer is conversation with God.

■ ■ ■

The Lord is near to all who call upon Him, to all who call upon Him sincerely and in truth.

Psalm 145:18 AMP

$\mathcal{T}$he story is told of an old Scotsman who was quite ill. The family called for their minister. As the pastor entered the man's room and sat down, he noticed another chair on the opposite side of the bed. The pastor said, "Well, I see I'm not your first visitor for the day."

The old man looked up, puzzled for a moment, then realized that the pastor had noticed the empty chair drawn close to his bedside. "Well, pastor," he said, "let me tell you about that chair. Many years ago I found it difficult to pray, so one day I shared this problem with my pastor. He told me not to worry about kneeling or about placing myself in some pious posture. Instead, he said, 'Just sit down, put a chair opposite you, imagine Jesus sitting in it, and then talk with Him as you would a friend.'" The old Scot added, "I've been doing that ever since."

A short time later, the daughter of the old man called the minister to tell him her father had died very suddenly. She said, "I had just gone to lie down for an hour or two. He seemed to be sleeping so comfortably. When I went back he was gone. What was odd was that his hand was on the empty chair at the side of the bed. Isn't that strange?" The minister replied, "No, that's not so strange. I think I understand."[90]

It is not well for a man to pray cream and live skim milk.

■ ■ ■

But wilt thou know, O vain man,
that faith without works is dead?

James 2:20

$\mathcal{I}$ knelt to pray when day was done,
    And prayed, "O Lord bless everyone.
Lift from every saddened heart the pain,
    And let the sick be well again."

And then I woke another day,
    And carelessly went upon my way.
The whole day long I did not try
    To wipe a tear from any eye.

I did not try to share the load
    Of any brother on the road.
I did not even go to see
    The sick man just next door to me.

Yet once again when day was done,
    I prayed "O Lord bless everyone."
But as I prayed, unto my ear
    There came a voice that whispered clear,

"Pause, hypocrite, before you pray,
    Whom have you tried to bless today?
God's sweetest blessings always go,
    By hands which serve Him below."

And then I hid my face and cried,
    "Forgive me, God, for I have lied.
Let me but live another day,
    And I will live the way I pray!"[91]

— Anonymous

He who prays as he ought, will endeavor to live as he prays.

For those who live according to the flesh set their minds on the things of the flesh, but those who live according to the Spirit set their minds on the things of the Spirit.

Romans 8:5 NRSV

$\mathcal{A}$ few years ago, a cable-television program decided to test the compassion of the people in the city where the program originated. An actor was hired to fake a fainting spell on a busy street corner and lay "unconscious" on the ground until someone came to his aid. Out-of-the-way cameras recorded the reactions of those who passed by. Literally hundreds of people came within inches of the man — who, it should be noted, did not have the appearance of a street person. Most passersby gave him a quick glance and kept walking. Some took a longer look, but they also kept walking. No one wanted to get involved — not even by notifying a policeman who was standing on the next corner. Eventually the actor revived himself, since no one came to his aid.

A similar story is told in the Bible in Luke 10:30-37. A man was beaten and left for dead by robbers. Both a priest and a Levite saw him lying in the ditch, but crossed the road to avoid him. Then a Samaritan and whom the Jews despised, stopped, bandaged his wounds, took him to an inn, and paid his expenses.

We are presumptuous to pray that God will meet our needs, if we are unwilling to extend ourselves to meet the needs of others.

If we could hear Christ praying for us in the next room, we would have no fear. Yet distance makes no difference. He is praying for us.

We have an advocate with the Father, Jesus Christ the righteous.

1 John 2:1

𝒟. 𝓛. Moody told the story of a Chinese convert who gave this testimony: "I was down in a deep pit, half sunk in the mire, crying for someone to help me out. As I looked up I saw a venerable, gray-haired man looking down at me. I said, 'Can you help me out?' 'My son,' he replied, 'I am Confucius. If you had read my books and followed what I taught, you would never have fallen into this dreadful pit.'

"Then he was gone. Soon I saw another man coming. He bent over me with closed eyes and folded arms. 'My son,' Buddha said, 'forget about yourself. Get into a state of rest. Then, my child, you will be in a delicious state just as I am.' 'Yes,' I said, 'I will do that when I am above this mire. Can you help me out?' I looked and he was gone.

"I was beginning to sink into despair when I saw another figure above me. There were marks of suffering on His face. 'My child,' He said, 'what is the matter?' But before I could reply, He was down in the mire by my side. He folded His arms about me and lifted me up and then fed and rested me. When I was well He did not say, 'Shame on you for falling into that pit.' Instead He said, 'We will walk on together now,' and we have been walking together until this day."[92]

No one can pray for you with greater insight or compassion than Jesus — and the Bible says He is continually making intercession to the Father on our behalf!

They who have steeped
their souls in prayer
can every anguish
calmly bear.

*He went away again the second time,
and prayed, saying, O my Father, if
this cup may not pass away from me,
except I drink it, thy will be done.*

Matthew 26:42

*A*dmiral James Kelly, the navy's chief of chaplains, tells how the members of the *Pueblo* crew — taken captive by the North Koreans — began to pray more and more frequently as the weary months of their imprisonment dragged on.

At mealtimes, the men would bow their heads slightly and thank God for the food before them. If Communist guards spotted them, however, the guards would scream, "This is not a church! This food is a gift from the Democratic People's Republic of North Korea!"

At night, the men dared not kneel beside their bunks, so they prayed as they were lying on their backs. Instead of praying to the Lord by name, they referred to Him as COMMWORLDFLT, which stood for "Commander of the world's fleets." These sailors felt they were making contact with the Supreme Commander of all things, and they stood firm in their belief that they were under His protection and care.[93]

Regardless of our circumstances, even when we cannot pray openly, God looks at our hearts. Whatever language we may use, whatever words are spoken, He hears us when our hearts are praying.

No prayer of adoration will ever soar higher than a simple cry: "I love You, God."

■ ■ ■

And though you have not seen Him, you love Him, and though you do not see Him now, but believe in Him, you greatly rejoice with joy inexpressible and full of glory.

1 Peter 1:8 NASB

$\mathcal{A}$ woman was very fearful about the outcome of the surgery she faced. Doctors had not been able to discover the reason for her symptoms, and cancer seemed a real possibility. To add to her concern, she had little in savings, and being self-employed, had no insurance or paid sick leave.

As her day of surgery drew closer, she found herself reading her Bible more and more frequently. A passage in Habakkuk puzzled her. The prophet obviously knew his nation was about to be invaded and ravaged, but he said, "Though the fig tree may not blossom, nor fruit be on the vines; though the labor of the olive may fail, and the fields yield no food; though the flock may be cut off from the fold, and there be no herd in the stalls — Yet I will rejoice in the LORD" (Habakkuk 3:17,18 NKJV). She began to reflect on the fact that God was always with her and always loved her. Instead of a request for healing, finances, or peace, her main prayer became simply, "I love You, too! I love You, too!"

As it turned out, surgeons removed a benign cyst. Her recovery passed quickly. Friends helped with meals, laundry, housecleaning, errands, and even a mortgage payment. She reflected later, "This experience made my love for God grow deeper. And that was far more important than a good medical report."[94]

If you are facing a burdensome situation today, reflect on God's love for you. Remember His faithfulness in the past. Then, with joy in your heart, tell God how much you love Him.

I do not pray for success. I ask for faithfulness.

And I will betroth you to Me in faithfulness. Then you will know the Lord.

Hosea 2:20 NASB

$\mathcal{K}$ari Torjesen Malcom, the daughter of missionaries, was interred in a Chinese prison camp during World War II. Only a teenager, she found herself a nameless Westerner, number "16," who was given a small space on a bare floor and reminded daily of her lack of freedom by a wall, a moat, and an electric barbed-wire fence. She met with other prisoners daily at noon to pray for freedom, but as time passed, the enemy seemed larger, and God smaller.

Kari desperately pleaded with God to reveal Himself to her. She said, "God answered my prayer and spoke to me as I searched the Bible.... Gradually it dawned on me that there was just one thing the enemy could not take from me. They had bombed our home, killed my father...but...they could not touch my relationship to my God."

With this revelation, Kari found it increasingly difficult to join her friends for prayer. There was more to life than just getting out of prison. The first day she missed the prayer meeting, a friend taunted her, "So we aren't good enough for you anymore, eh?" Even her peer group had been stripped away from her. Her last bit of security was peeled away. Kari said, "It was only then that I was able to pray the prayer that changed my life: 'Lord, I am willing to stay in this prison for the rest of my life if only I may know You.' At that moment I was free."[95]

Pray devoutly, but hammer stoutly.

Therefore, my beloved, be steadfast, immovable, always excelling in the work of the Lord....

1 Corinthians 15:58 NRSV

*O*n a trip across the Atlantic, Dwight L. Moody had an opportunity to help the crew and other volunteers put out a fire in the hold of the ship. A friend said to Moody as they stood in the bucket line, "Let's go up to the other end of the ship and pray."

Moody, a commonsense evangelist, said, "No, sir, we will stand right here, pass buckets, and pray hard all the time we are doing so!"

To be a praying Christian does not mean we pray occasionally, but that we pray continually — wherever we are and in whatever we are doing. Just as:

- no one can live by taking a breath only once in a while, or survive by taking only a sip of water once a week...
- no person can read by a light that flickers on and off...
- no sailor can steer his course with only an occasional puff of wind....

So too, with prayer and the Christian life. A Christian cannot maintain a healthy spiritual life by praying occasionally. We must pray always, in all things, in spite of all circumstances.[96]

Pray to God, but row for the shore.

Whatever you do, do your work heartily, as for the Lord rather than for men.

Colossians 3:23 NASB

$\mathcal{A}$ man once dreamed of building a playground in a ghetto neighborhood. He approached the owners of an apartment complex, who gave him permission to build, but offered no help. As he walked through the complex one day, he met a little girl. He shared his dream with her and she immediately ran to her apartment and returned with a thick stack of crayon sketches. She already shared his vision! Her drawings showed him the playground she wanted — one with a slide, lots of swings, and monkey bars. She showed him the exact spot where she wanted it built, and then she said, "I've been praying for this a long time!"

The man told her he would need lots of help to turn the dream into a reality, and the little girl nodded in agreement. In the coming weeks, she tirelessly slipped fliers under doors, and made appointments for the man to speak to parents and teachers. Word spread. Several companies donated materials. The little girl convinced architects and fund-raisers to help build her dream. When construction started, hundreds of volunteers showed up to help. Soon, there was a playground![97]

Are you willing to work for what you request? It may be the very key to your receiving God's best.

Don't pray for tasks suited to your capacity. Pray for capacity suited to your tasks.

But to us, O Lord, be merciful, for we have waited for you. Be our strength each day and our salvation in the time of trouble.

Isaiah 33:2 TLB

*D*oes it seem to you that the only miracle stories you hear occurred in remote African villages or obscure Chinese provinces? Is God visibly active only on the mission field? Steven Mosley, author of *If Only God Would Answer*, believes the reason we hear more stories from missionary ventures than local churches is, "God is most active when we are reaching out most. He stretches out when we stretch out.

"Consider the life of George Mueller. He wrote an entire book of answers to specific prayer requests he made while living in complacent Victorian England. Müeller was stretched — he was seeking to meet the needs of two thousand orphans. In remote China, Hudson Taylor was given needed funds or had personnel needs met without ever making an appeal to any human being. Taylor was stretched — sharing the Gospel where it had not been preached before. Brother Andrew, 'God's Smuggler,' had an abundance of answered prayers. He, too, was stretched — devoting his life to taking Bibles behind the iron curtain."

Mosley has concluded, "God is most active in the thick of it."[98]

Are you asking God today to help you meet your heart's desires, or are you asking Him how you might help Him meet *His* heart's desires?

Oh, do not pray for easy lives. Pray to be stronger men.

Those who hope in the Lord will renew their strength.

Isaiah 40:31 NIV

$\mathcal{W}$hen Martin Luther began the work that became the Great Reformation, his friend Myconius said, "I can best help where I am. I will remain and pray while you toil."

Then, one night Myconius dreamed that Jesus approached him and showed him His hands and feet, wounded by His crucifixion. He looked into the eyes of his Savior and heard Jesus say to him, "Follow Me." Jesus led him to a mountaintop and pointed eastward. Myconius looked and saw a plain stretching away to the horizon. It was dotted with thousands and thousands of white sheep. One man was trying to shepherd the great flock. Myconius recognized him as his friend, Luther. The Savior then pointed westward and Myconius saw a great field of standing corn. Only one reaper was trying to harvest it all. The lonely laborer was obviously exhausted, but he persisted. Myconius recognized the solitary reaper, again, it was Luther.

"It is not enough that I should pray," said Myconius when he awoke. "The sheep must be shepherded; the field must be reaped. Here am I; send me." He immediately sought out Luther and volunteered to serve in whatever capacity Luther desired.[99]

Today, are you praying to help, or to be of help?

We are living in
dangerous times
and if there was
ever a time when
we need to pray,
it's now.

The end of all things is near.
Therefore be clear minded and
self-controlled so that you can pray.
1 Peter 4:7 NIV

When Evelyn Christenson, founder of United Prayer Ministries, arrived in El Salvador early one morning she discovered that three hours earlier, Communist rebels had knocked out all electricity in San Salvador. As she was driven into the city, everywhere Christenson looked she saw the signs of civil war: tanks rumbling in the streets, soldiers standing with guns cocked, ready to fire. That afternoon, on a street near the university where she was speaking, a car was blown up.

As she was being driven to the airport the next day, assailants rushed a taxi ahead of her and dragged out its occupants. Her driver careened around the besieged taxi and sped away. Christenson shot up a desperate prayer: "Oh, Father, protect us! Don't let them get us!" Immediately, she was calm and felt the Lord reassure her, "You don't have to pray that prayer. You *are* already protected by all that praying." Her mind turned to family, board members, and friends whom she knew were praying. Then she remembered the 1,000 prayer-clock members who were praying around the clock, and the women at the previous day's meeting in Guatemala, who had formed a prayer chain to pray for her safety in El Salvador. *Yes...all that praying!* she thought, rejoicing.[100]

In times of danger, there's no greater source of protection than God, no more effective recourse than prayer.

More can be done by prayer than anything else. Prayer is our greatest weapon.

Wherefore take unto you the whole armour of God...praying always with all prayer and supplication.
Ephesians 6:13,18

In Diamonds in the Dust, Joni Eareckson Tada reveals that her bed is the place she prays best. Because of her paralysis, she is forced to lie down early each evening. Sometimes, a friend comes over to sit on the edge of her bed and pray with her. One night, she writes, her friend "sprang a surprise and brought a small short-wave radio.... She flicked it on and tuned in Trans World Radio from the Caribbean. Another jiggle of the knob and we picked up someone leading a Bible study over station HCJB in Ecuador. A little more fiddling and we pulled in the BBC from Hong Kong. Together, my friend and I tuned in to the world."

They used the radio as a springboard for prayer. Tada says, "We covered the planet, yet didn't budge beyond my bed.... Just as the voices of people around the world reached us through short-wave, my prayers, immediate and instant, were touching others. That very second, godly grace was being applied as I prayed, and I didn't even have to leave my room."[101]

Where will you travel in prayer today? What spiritual battles will you wage in faraway places? As you pray, remember these words of Bernard of Clairvaux: "However great may be the temptation, if we know how to use the weapon of prayer well we shall come off conquerors at last, for prayer is more powerful than all the devils."[102]

A good man's prayers
will from the deepest
dungeon climb heaven's
height, and bring
a blessing down.

Thou art my hope, O Lord God...
[Thou] shalt quicken me again,
and shalt bring me up again
from the depths of the earth.
Psalm 71:5,20

*B*uddy's busy day was over. He was actually ready to kneel by his bed and join his father in bedtime prayers. He prayed about the many activities of his day, thanking God for the ability to catch a lizard and pass a spelling test. Then listened as his father prayed for his health, safety, and protection from evil. The customary "amen" was said and Buddy was tucked into bed. Before his father left the room, however, he sat up to ask, "Daddy, how high did we pray tonight? Did our prayers get all the way to Heaven?"

His father, accustomed to fielding such difficult questions, assured Buddy that God had heard their every word, since He always hears anything we pray. Buddy fell back onto his pillow and was asleep almost before his father left the room.

Daddy, however, pondered his son's question for some time. He was reminded that the Scriptures tell us we are not forgiven unless we first forgive others, and that Jesus once told a man to leave his offering at an altar and first go to make amends with a person he had offended.

The daddy realized there are some things that can hinder our prayers. His son's question was not really that far off.[103]

How high did you pray today?

I have been driven
many times to my knees
by the overwhelming
conviction that I had
nowhere else to go.

*The eternal God is your refuge
and dwelling place, and underneath
are the everlasting arms.*

Deuteronomy 33:27 AMP

$\mathcal{M}$ary George, known to her friends as "the girl of prayer," tells of a time when she, her six sisters, and a brother were facing eviction. Mary's parents had died, and the owners of the house in which she and her siblings were living wanted to convert the home into an apartment house. The house itself was in dire need of repair. The roof leaked, the water heater was broken, and the ceilings were about to cave in. Mary wasn't at all sorry at the prospect of leaving the old house, but finding a house large enough for a family of eight, and more importantly, one they could afford, wasn't easy. They prayed and prayed, both individually and as a family.

Then, Mary felt led to ask about a house just a block away. She was told that a buyer was closing on the sale the next day. But later that same week, the owner phoned her to tell her that the buyer had backed out. The house was theirs. Unfortunately, it was in an equal state of disrepair to the house they were vacating. Mary recalled, "The next day we signed the lease, and word got around the neighborhood how God took care of the Georges. Immediately, neighbors and friends volunteered to help us clean and do repairs, and make the house livable."[104]

The best place to go when you think you have no place to turn, is the throne room of Heaven.

True prayer brings a person's will into accordance with God's will, not the other way around.

The labor of the righteous leads to life.
Proverbs 10:16 NKJV

*A*n overweight man decided it was time to shed a few pounds. One morning, however, he arrived at work carrying a gigantic coffee cake. His co-workers scolded him, but he smiled and said, "This is a very *special* coffee cake. I drove by the bakery this morning and there in the window were a host of goodies. I felt this was no accident, so I prayed, 'Lord, if you want me to have one of these delicious coffee cakes, let me have a parking place directly in front of the bakery.' And sure enough, the eighth time around the block, there it was!"[105]

In *A Lamp for My Feet*, Elisabeth Elliot writes about the relationship in prayer between our will and God's will: "Does prayer work? The answer to that depends on one's definition of work. It is necessary to know what a thing is in order to judge whether it works. It would be senseless, for example, to say that if a screwdriver fails to drive nails into a board it doesn't 'work.' A screwdriver works very well for driving screws. Often we expect to arrange things according to our whims by praying about them, and when the arrangement fails to materialize we conclude that prayer doesn't work. God wants our willing cooperation in the bringing in of his kingdom. If 'Thy kingdom come' is an honest prayer, we will seek to ask for whatever contributes to that end."[106]

225

We can expect
big trouble
when we try
to answer
our own prayers.

■ ■ ■

O Jehovah, answer my prayers...
for I am in deep trouble. Quick!
Come and save me.

Psalm 69:16,17 TLB

"*H*ave you, perchance, found a diamond pendant? I feel certain I lost it last night in your theater," a woman phoned to ask the theater manager.

"Not that I know, madam," the manager said, "but let me ask some of my employees. Please hold the line for a minute while I make inquiry. If it hasn't been found, we certainly will make a diligent search for it."

Returning to the phone a few minutes later, the manager said, "I have good news for you! The diamond pendant has been found!"

There was no reply, however, to his news. "Hello! Hello!" he called into the phone, and then he heard the dial tone. The woman who made the inquiry about the lost diamond pendant had failed to wait for his answer. She had not given her name and attempts to trace her call were unsuccessful. The pendant was eventually sold to raise money for the theater.[107]

We are often like this woman when we make our requests to God. We fail to wait on the Lord to hear His reply. Instead, we rush ahead impatiently, having no idea he has a great blessing ready to give us, if only we'd slow down long enough to receive it!

Genuine prayer is never "good works," an exercise or pious attitude, but it is always the prayer of a child to a Father.

But Jesus replied, "Let the little children come to me, and don't prevent them. For of such is the Kingdom of Heaven."

Matthew 19:14 TLB

It was nearly 11 PM by the time two women left a parent's meeting at their children's school, which was located some 25 miles from their homes. As they neared their car, they noticed three youths running from the parking area, laughing. "It seems we got here just in time," the driver said, and was glad when her engine sputtered to life. "There's a shortcut my husband takes," she said, hoping to cut some time off of their drive, since it was so late.

Forty minutes later, they were lost. Then, their headlights began to flicker and the engine lost power. "Shall we walk and see if we can find a phone?" the driver asked. "Let's pray first," the other woman suggested. Together they prayed, "Lord, guide us to help."

They walked to a crossroad and saw a distant porch light. When a man answered their knock, they told him their problem. He said, "I'm a mechanic. Maybe I can help." When he checked the car, he said, "Some joker exchanged batteries with you. You have a golf-cart battery in your car! This may sound strange to you but just today I brought a new battery home from my garage. I'll put it in for you if you like." Before long, the car was repaired and the Lord had one more surprise. Friends visiting the man and his wife were from their hometown. They were just about to leave, so the two women followed them home![108]

God is always available to lead us and guide us. He can see the road ahead and knows what we'll be needing, He prepares it, then when we ask, He leads us right to the answer we need. All we have to do is ask!

Prayer is the opening
of your heart to God
as to a friend.
You speak to Him,
and He speaks back
— if you'll but listen.

Be still, and know that I am God!
Psalm 46:10

" *I*f you want to hear God's voice and you are uncertain," Corrie ten Boom has written, "then remain in His presence until He changes this uncertainty. Often much can happen during this waiting for the Lord. Sometimes He changes pride into humility; doubt into faith and peace; sometimes lust into purity. The Lord can and will do it.

"We must also understand that sometimes the silence of the Lord is His way of letting us grow, just as a mother allows her child to fall and get up again when he is learning to walk. If at times God allows a conflict, it may be His way of training us.

"Psalm 32:8 says: 'I will instruct thee and teach thee in the way which thou shalt go: I will guide thee with mine eye.' Could it be clearer? And Psalm 48:14 says: 'For this God is our God for ever and ever: he will be our guide even unto death.'

"It is not at all difficult for the Lord to guide us. And asking things of God gives us a wonderful opportunity to have fellowship with Him. What a comfort it is to know that before we were born, God made His plan for us. He gave us our talents and qualities, and He most certainly will not waste them."[109]

We possess a divine artillery that silences the enemy and inflicts upon him the damage he would inflict upon us.

■ ■ ■

The weapons of our warfare
are not carnal but mighty through
God for pulling down strongholds.
2 Corinthians 10:4 NKJV

One of the two most famous legions in the Roman army was the Militine Legion, also known as the Thundering Legion. The nickname was given by the philosopher-emperor, Marcus Aurelius in 176 AD, during a military campaign against the Germans.

In their march northward, the Romans were encircled by precipitous mountains which were occupied by their enemies. In addition, due to a drought, they were tormented by great thirst. Then, a member of the Praetorian Guard informed the emperor that the Militine Legion was made up of Christians who believed in the power of prayer. Although he himself had been a great persecutor of the Church, the emperor said, "Let them pray then." The soldiers bowed on the ground and earnestly sought God in the name of Jesus Christ to deliver them.

They had scarcely risen from their knees when a great thunderstorm arose. The storm drove their enemies from their strongholds and into their arms, where they pleaded for mercy. The storm also provided water to drink and ended the drought. The emperor renamed them "Thundering Legion," and subsequently abated some of his persecution of the Christians in Rome.[110]

Prayer and deliverance go hand in hand!

Prayer is the preface to the book of Christian living; the text of the new life sermon; the girding on of the armor for battle.

■ ■ ■

Put on the whole armor of God, that you may be able to stand against the wiles of the devil... praying always with all prayer and supplication in the Spirit.

Ephesians 6:11,18 NKJV

*F*or seven horrible years, Jeremiah Denton was a prisoner of war in North Vietnam. He was in solitary confinement for most of that time. As one of the highest ranking American captives, he was subjected to grueling torture. Still, he not only survived but was elected as one of Alabama's United States senators.

How did Denton cope with the tedium and pain of his captivity? On many occasions, he stated that one of his basic survival skills was quoting passages he had memorized from the Bible. Internalized Scriptures were his unseen sword to fend off the cruelest weapons of the enemy. By inwardly focusing on the power of God to sustain and strengthen him, he was able to rise above his circumstances. Memorized Scriptures became his prayers.[111]

When we meditate upon God and His Word, recalling His many promises and acts of faithfulness, our faith grows and our fears dissolve. David understood this well. Many times, in his attempts to escape the wrath of King Saul he recalled the greatness of God, and as he did, he found himself strengthened.

When we fix our minds and spirits upon God's nature, His presence with us, and His Word, our prayers change. They become more faith-filled, more hope-filled, and more love-filled. And in turn, so do we.

When we depend on man, we get what man can do; when we depend on prayer, we get what God can do.

Now to him who is able to do immeasurably more than all we ask or imagine, according to his power that is at work within us.

Ephesians 3:20 NIV

Several men went on a mission trip to Haiti. While they were there, they met a nineteen-year-old youth who deeply loved Christ. He impressed them so greatly that they invited him to visit them in the United States and paid for his trip. The young Haitian felt as if he was in another world. He had never slept between sheets, had never had three meals in one day, had never used indoor plumbing, and had never tasted a hamburger.

By the end of his six-week visit, the young man had made many friends, so his hosts held a farewell dinner in his honor. Several members of the group offered warm parting remarks. Then they asked the youth if he would like to say something. "Yes," he replied, "I would. I want to thank you so much for inviting me here. I have really enjoyed this time in the United States. But I am also very glad to be going home. You have so much in America that I'm beginning to lose my grip on my day-to-day dependency on Christ."[112]

Are you truly relying on the Lord to lead you, to give you wisdom, and meet your needs, or are you trusting in your own ability? His desire is that we rely completely on Him. Only then can He provide everything He desires to give us, because then, will we be open to receive it.

Prayer is a powerful thing because God has bound it to Himself.

And I will do whatever you ask in my name, so that the Son may bring glory to the Father.

John 14:13 NIV

 $\mathcal{F}$ ay Angus has said about prayer: "Without circumventing scriptural directionals, encouragements and admonitions...the bottom line of prayer is to pray. When we do, the power of Heaven picks up momentum to change our lives.

"Much as we try to put Him there, God is not on trial; the good news is that neither is man. Jesus Christ stood in the docket on our behalf.

"If the answers to our prayers depended upon our worth, they would never be answered — they would never even be heard. Through the righteousness of Christ, they are.

"We tend to stroke prayer like a lucky rabbit's foot, and seek God's fleece rather than His face.

"We try to manipulate His will to ours and sometimes call it faith. We push forward in the arrogance of our own stoic determination, limited by our finite vision, rather than pull back in the simple trust of His infinite plan.

"We expect Him to change the sovereignty of His omnipotent heart, instead of humbly asking Him to give us a heart willing to be changed.

"'Be still, and know that I am God' (Psalm 46:10 KJV) means, 'Relax, let God be God.'"[113]

Prayer serves as an
edge and border
to preserve
the web of life
from unraveling.

■ ■ ■

Thou hast enclosed me behind and
before, and laid Thy hand upon me.
Psalm 139:5 NASB

$\mathscr{I}$t was only four days until her seventeenth birthday, but this year there would be no celebration. It was the depth of the Great Depression, and her father was dying. Her mother prayed as the children knelt around his bed, but the girl wondered whether anyone was listening. *Was God near enough to hear our prayer? Did He take any notice of our situation?*

It rained the day of the funeral. Only her mother's friends came. The friends of her father didn't bother. The girl, who worked as a maid, had to borrow a dress for the occasion. When she returned home, a sense of desolation nearly overwhelmed her. Her mother, who had been silent for three days, went into the kitchen, picked up a broom, and began to sweep.

Years later the girl would write, "I cannot explain how that action and the soft whisk-whisk sound gave me courage to go on. My mother was now the head of the house, and we followed. We did not sit down and ask, 'What next? What will we do?' Our home was mortgaged and my father's lawyer stole her property. She walked out of his office a penniless widow with seven children, ages eight to eighteen. Later someone asked my mother how she had stood it. Her answer was simple: 'I prayed.'"[114]

Prayer is God's way of doing God's will.

So the man of God interceded with the Lord, and the king's hand was restored and became as it was before.

1 Kings 13:6 NIV

Soon after the birth of the Solidarity movement in Poland, Father Jerzy Popieluszko preached among the striking workers in Warsaw's huge steelworks. When martial law was imposed, he made a foray into the night to spread Christmas peace to the soldiers. Then, he instituted a monthly "Mass for the Homeland," dedicated to victims of the repressive communist regime. Tens of thousands attended these services.

Father Jerzy's influence and popularity did not escape the notice of communist officials. The secret police followed him. He received unsigned, threatening letters. On the first anniversary of imposed martial law, a pipe bomb sailed into his apartment and exploded. Then, after celebrating a special mass and giving a homily entitled "Overcome Evil with Good," he disappeared. His body was found in the Vistula River.

Word of Father Jerzy's death came as 50,000 people were listening, in tears, to a tape of his final sermon. In a second, people were down on their knees, crying loudly. And then...three times they repeated after the priest, "And forgive us our trespasses as we forgive them that trespass against us." The crowd could forgive! Father Antoni Lewek, one of the priests present, said, "It was a Christian answer to the unchristian deed of the murderers."[115]

Forgiveness gives us tremendous power in prayer. When we forgive, releasing those who have hurt or offended us to God, He is then free to deal with them, and work a healing in our hearts.

We cannot separate our prayer from how we treat other people.

If therefore you are presenting your offering at the altar, and there remember that your brother has something against you, leave your offering there before the altar, and go your way; first be reconciled to your brother, and then come and present your offering.

Matthew 5:23,24 NASB

*L*ate one night a salesman drove into an unfamiliar city. He tried to get a room in a hotel, but the clerk informed him that there was no vacancy. In fact, he said he doubted if any hotel in the city had a vacancy, since several major conferences were being held in town. Disappointed, the man prepared to leave the hotel lobby, when a distinguished gentleman offered to share his room with him. Gratefully, the weary traveler accepted his kindness.

Before retiring, the hospitable man knelt and prayed aloud. In his prayers, he mentioned the stranger by name and asked the Lord to bless him. Upon awakening the next morning, he told his guest that it was his habit to read the Bible and commune with God at the beginning of each day. He asked the salesman if he would like to join him. The Holy Spirit had been speaking to his heart, and when his host tactfully confronted him with the message of Jesus Christ, he gladly received Jesus as his Savior.

As the two were about to part, they exchanged business cards. The new believer was amazed when he read, "William Jennings Bryan, Secretary of State."[116]

We do pray
for mercy, and
that same prayer
doth teach us all
to render the
deeds of mercy.

■ ■ ■

Blessed are the merciful:
for they shall obtain mercy.

Matthew 5:7

Christians in the Orthodox Church, and many other mainline denominations, use a prayer called the "Jesus Prayer." It is often voiced in the rhythm of breathing. As such, it is a prayer that becomes for many a means of "praying without ceasing." The words are simple, but they cover everything we truly need: *Lord Jesus Christ, Son of God, have mercy on us.*

Some Christians become critical of repetitious prayers. Jesus, however, did not preach against repetition. He preached against the use of *vain* repetition — repetition for the sake of appearing holy to others. A prayer voiced from the heart, filled with meaning to the speaker, is never a vain prayer.

The Very Reverend Kenneth R. Waldron, a priest of both the Ukrainian Orthodox Church and the Anglican Church, underwent surgery. He wrote, "The last moment of consciousness before the anesthetic took over, I heard my surgeon repeating in a whisper, GOSPODI POMILUY, GOSPODI POMILUY, GOSPODI POMILUY." He was praying, "Lord, have mercy on us." To Reverend Waldron, it was a tremendous comfort to drift into unconsciousness hearing those words from the lips of his surgeon.[117]

No doubt most people would find such a prayer comforting, especially prayed on their behalf!

The Lord's Prayer... may be committed to memory quickly, but it is slowly learned by heart.

Our Father which art in heaven, Hallowed be thy name.

Matthew 6:9

A minister had returned to school to work on his graduate degree. As he neared the end of his studies, he began to actively search for a pastorate. He had been serving as interim minister at a small church, which had invited him to become their permanent pastor, but he felt that he could attain a better position with his graduate degree. Soon he was invited to visit a number of larger, more prestigious churches. For some reason, however, he was not invited to become the pastor of any of these churches. He became anxious about why he wasn't chosen, and was puzzled about what he might do to turn things around.

One day at a prayer seminar, he received new insight into the importance of both thanksgiving and listening as part of prayer. He decided to try both. He began to spend his prayer times thanking God for His many blessings, including the church he had been pastoring. Then, as he listened for God to speak, he realized that he truly enjoyed the work he had been doing. He accepted the call to the little church and was very happy there for many years.[118]

The Lord's prayer calls us to pray, "Thy will be done. Thy kingdom come." We may find if we pray with a thankful and listening heart, His kingdom has already come and His will is being done — in us!

If you can't pray
as you want to,
pray as you can.
God knows
what you mean.

"Lord, help me!"

Matthew 15:25 NIV

𝘔any years ago, on a bitterly cold day in February, a little boy about ten years old was standing barefoot in front of a shoe store in New York City. A woman riding up the street in a beautiful carriage saw him and immediately ordered her driver to stop. Richly dressed, she alighted from her carriage and quickly went to the boy. "My little fellow, why are you looking so earnestly in that window?"

"I was asking God to give me a pair of shoes," he replied, shivering. The woman took him by the hand and went into the store. She asked the proprietor of the store to assign a clerk to her and requested half a dozen pair of socks. She also asked for a basin of water and a towel. When he brought them to her, she took the boy to the back of the store, removed her gloves, knelt down, washed his grimy feet, and dried them with the towel. She then had him put on a pair of socks and they returned to the main part of the store, where she bought him a pair of shoes. As they parted she said, "I hope, my little fellow, that you are more comfortable."

He caught her hand and with tears in his eyes, replied to her, "Are you God's wife?"

The best way to remember people is in prayer.

Keep praying earnestly for all Christians everywhere.

Ephesians 6:18 TLB

$\mathcal{B}$ack in 1993, a group called AD 2000 United Prayer Track came up with an innovative idea. In order to help realize their goal of "a church for every people and the Gospel for every person by AD 2000," they established a program called "Praying through the Window."

The "window," referred to an area on the globe from 10 degrees to 40 degrees north of the equator, from North Africa and southern Spain eastward to Japan and the northern Philippines. More than 2.5 billion people live in this area, where the most prominent religions are Buddhism, Islam, and Hinduism. For the entire month of October 1993, and again in 1995, millions of Christians from around the world prayed for the people in the 10/40 window.

The goal was that new churches might be established and new missionaries sent to these areas. In 1993 alone, the number of churches in Albania grew from 50 to more than 300, and the number of Christian fellowship groups formed daily in India rose from an average of 3 to 17.[119]

In praying for people around the world, we are called to remember not only those who already *are* believers, that they might grow in their faith and be equipped to endure persecution and hardships, but we are called to pray for *new* believers to enter the Kingdom!

He prayeth best, who loveth best.

■ ■ ■

Dear friends, since God so loved us,
we also ought to love one another.

1 John 4:11 NIV

J. Hudson Taylor, founder of the China Inland Mission, prepared himself for missionary service by doing Gospel work among the poor in London. One night, a man asked him to come and pray for his sick wife. He had sought a priest, but had been told he would have to pay eighteen pence, which he did not have. He didn't even have money to buy a loaf of bread.

Taylor gladly went with him, but was conscience-stricken. He was living on a starvation diet himself, but he did have one coin in his pocket — a half crown. He thought, *If only I had two shillings and a sixpence, instead of this half crown, I would give these poor people a shilling.* Upon arriving at the man's tenement, he was overcome at seeing the sunken cheeks of the children and the exhausted mother who lay with a tiny infant by her side.

Taylor spoke to them, trying to bring comfort and encouragement, but inside he cried, "You hypocrite! telling these people about a kind and loving Father in heaven, and not prepared yourself to trust Him without half a crown." Before he could pray, he dug deep into his pocket for the half crown and gave it to the man. "And how the joy came back in full flood tide to my heart!... Not only was the poor woman's life saved, but my life as fully realized had been saved too."[120]

Men may spurn our appeals, reject our message, oppose our arguments, despise our persons, but they are helpless against our prayers.

For God is my witness, whom I serve with my spirit in the gospel of his Son, that without ceasing I make mention of you always in my prayers.

Romans 1:9

$\mathscr{B}$efore the surrender of Weinsberg, the women of that besieged city asked the enemy to allow them to leave the city carrying their most precious possessions with them. Permission was granted. To the astonishment of the victors, the women of Weinsberg, displaying both shrewdness and love, came plodding through the city gates with their husbands, sons, and brothers on their shoulders![121]

How wise we are to carry our dear ones out of sin, away from evil, and far from the carnal world on the shoulders of our prayers. During one of D. L. Moody's services in London, this happened in a profound way. A father and mother voiced great distress about their son, who had given up God's ways and run away to the bush of Australia. They asked the vast congregation to pray for their son. That night, some 20,000 believers voiced prayers on his behalf.

Later, the parents learned that at the very hour of that prayer, their son had been riding through the Australian bush into town, a day's ride from his camp. As he rode, the Spirit of the Lord convicted him of his sin. Dismounting, he knelt and asked God for forgiveness. When he reached town, he wired the news of his repentance to his mother and asked her if he might come home. Her reply was cabled immediately, "Come home at once!"[122]

"Christian! seek not yet repose," Hear thy guardian angel say; Thou art in the midst of foes, "Watch and pray."

Take heed, watch and pray.

Mark 13:33 NKJV

*L*awrence Cunningham sometimes visits a nearby Trappist monastery. For him, the best part of the monastic day comes in the two hours between 3:15 and 5:15 AM, a time set aside for vigilance: "O watchman, what of the night?" He writes:

"I think of those who lie awake staring at the ceiling, worrying about money or children or the nagging pain in the belly that keeps them from sleep. I think of those who work in all-night diners or convenience stores.... Have the bars closed?... Have the street hustlers and the young-but-so-old hookers quit the streets yet? Have the dopers found some rest? Are the street people now snoring in wine-drenched quiet? Is it easy for the cops in their patrol cars and the firemen in their stations and the nurses in the ER room? Have the sirens silenced a bit? Do the people on death row sleep easily amid the coughs and groans of the prison population?... Is it now too late for the rapist and housebreaker?... Are the milkers and produce buyers and long-haul truckers at work?... Are my kids and wife and friends and students safe?"[123]

Each question becomes a prayer to Cunningham, who agrees with what Thomas Merton wrote: "The more we are alone with God, the more we are with one another in darkness." It is always a good time to watch and pray!

I have so much to do today that I shall spend the first three hours in prayer.

*I rise before dawn and cry for help;
I have put my hope in your word.*

Psalm 119:147 NIV

None of us automatically has time to pray. Each of us must make time for prayer — carving a time out of our day and setting it aside as a sacred appointment that cannot be changed, and must not be delayed. Consider this Japanese version of the 23rd Psalm as you set aside our prayer time for today:

The Lord is my pace setter...I shall not rush.

He makes me stop for quiet intervals.

He provides me with images of stillness which restore my serenity.

He leads me in the way of efficiency through calmness of mind and His guidance is peace.

Even though I have a great many things to accomplish each day, I will not fret,

for His presence is here.

His timelessness, His all-importance will keep me in balance.

He prepares refreshment and renewal in the midst of my activity by anointing my mind with the oils of tranquillity.

My cup of joyous energy overflows.

Truly harmony and effectiveness shall be the fruits of my hours,

for I shall walk in the pace of my Lord and dwell in His house for ever.[124]

Do not face a day until you have faced God.

O God...early will I seek thee: my soul thirsteth for thee, my flesh longeth for thee in a dry and thirsty land, where no water is.

Psalm 63:1

$\mathcal{H}$ow hollow our excuse sounds when we say, "I just didn't have time to spend with You today, Lord." Perhaps our not seeking Him is the reason so many of us have difficulty finding His answers.

I got up early one morning
And rushed right into the day;
I had so much to accomplish
I didn't have time to pray.

Troubles just tumbled about me
And heavier came each task.
Why doesn't God help me, I wondered.
He answered, "You didn't ask."

I tried to come into God's presence,
I used all my keys at the lock.
God gently and lovingly chided,
"Why child, you didn't knock."

I wanted to see joy and beauty,
But the day toiled on grey and bleak,
I called on the Lord for the reason —
He said, "You didn't seek."

I woke up early this morning
And paused before entering the day.
I had so much to accomplish
That I had to take time to pray. [125]

— Unknown

There are moments when, whatever be the attitude of the body, the soul is on its knees.

■ ■ ■

My soul waits in silence for God only; from Him is my salvation.

Psalm 62:1 NASB

In Glorious Intruder, Joni Eareckson Tada writes about Diane, who suffers from multiple sclerosis: "In her quiet sanctuary, Diane turns her head slightly on the pillow toward the corkboard on the wall. Her eyes scan each thumbtacked card and list. Each photo. Every torn piece of paper carefully pinned in a row. The stillness is broken as Diane begins to murmur. She is praying.

"Some would look at Diane — stiff and motionless — and shake their heads...'What a shame. Her life has no meaning. She can't really do anything.' But Diane is confident, convinced her life is significant. Her labor of prayer counts. She moves mountains that block the paths of missionaries. She helps open the eyes of the spiritually blind in southeast Asia. She pushes back the kingdom of darkness that blackens the alleys and streets of the gangs in east LA. She aids homeless mothers, single parents, abused children, despondent teenagers, handicapped boys, and the dying and forgotten old people in the nursing home down the street from where she lives. Diane is on the front lines, advancing the Gospel of Christ, holding up weak saints, inspiring doubting believers, energizing other prayer warriors, and delighting her Lord and Savior."[126]

If you want to know about God, there is only one way to do it: Get down on your knees.

*If any of you lacks wisdom,
let him ask of God, who gives to all
liberally and without reproach,
and it will be given to him.*

James 1:5 NKJV

F. B. Meyer has written, "I knelt by my bed, with the door of my room locked, and resolved that I would not sleep until I had settled the matter and surrendered everything to Jesus. It seemed as though Jesus was by my side and that I took from my pocket a large bunch of keys. From that bunch I took one tiny key, which I kept, and then held to Jesus the bunch with the one missing. 'Here are the keys of my life,' I said. He looked at me sadly and asked, 'Are all there?' 'All but one tiny one, to a small cupboard. It is so small that it cannot amount to anything.' He replied, 'Child, if you cannot trust Me with everything, you cannot trust Me with anything....

"At last I said, 'Lord, I cannot give the key, but I am willing to have You come and take it.' It was as I expected. I seemed to hold out my hand, and He came and opened the fingers and took the key from me. Then He went straight to that cupboard, unlocked and opened it and saw there a thing that was terrible and hideous. He said, 'This must go out. You must never go that way again.' And the moment He took the thing from me, He took the desire for it out of my soul, and I began to hate it. Then I yielded myself absolutely to Him and said, 'From this night I want You to do as You will

If you find it hard to stand for Jesus, try kneeling first.

*Daniel, who is one of the exiles from
Judah, pays no attention to you,
O king, or to the decree
you put in writing.
He still prays three times a day.*

Daniel 6:13 NIV

$\mathcal{G}$eorge Whitefield, the famous English evangelist, said, "O Lord, give me souls, or take my soul!"

Missionary Henry Martyn knelt on India's coral strands and cried out, "Here let me burn out for God."

David Brainerd, a missionary to the North American Indians (1718-1747) prayed, "Lord, to Thee I dedicate myself. O accept of me, and let me be Thine forever. Lord, I desire nothing else, I desire nothing more."

Thomas a'Kempis (1379-1471) prayed, "Give what Thou wilt, and how much Thou wilt, and when Thou wilt. Set me where Thou wilt and deal with me in all things, just as Thou wilt."

Dwight L. Moody prayed, "Use me then, my Savior, for whatever purpose and in whatever way Thou mayest require. Here is my poor heart, an empty vessel; fill it with Thy grace."

John McKenzie prayed as a young missionary candidate, "O Lord, send me to the darkest spot on earth!"

John Hunt, a missionary to the Fiji Islands, prayed upon his death bed, "Lord, save Fiji, save Fiji; save these people, O Lord; have mercy upon Fiji; save Fiji." [128]

What you pray today will determine how you live when you rise from your knees.

You will not stumble while on your knees.

■ ■ ■

Uphold my steps in Your paths,
That my footsteps may not slip.

Psalm 17:5 NKJV

In The Pursuit of Holiness, Jerry Bridges has written: "I still vividly recall how God first dealt with me over twenty-five years ago about complaining against Him. In response to His will, I had settled in San Diego, California, and had begun to look for a job. When several weeks went by without success, I mentally began to accuse God. 'After all, I gave up my plans to do His will and now He has let me down.' God graciously directed my attention to Job 34:18,19 NIV: 'Is he not the One who says to kings, "You are worthless," and to nobles, "You are wicked," who shows no partiality to princes and does not favor the rich over the poor, for they are all the work of his hands?'

"As soon as I read that passage I immediately fell to my knees confessing to Him my terrible sin of complaining and questioning His holiness. God mercifully forgave and the next day I received two job offers."[129]

If your life is not turning out the way you had planned...

If your day seems to be haphazard and out of control...

If your hour isn't as productive as you had desired...

If you can't seem to find peace...

It's time to pray.

Life's best outlook is a prayerful uplook.

■ ■ ■

*Giving thanks always for all things
unto God and the Father
in the name of our Lord Jesus Christ.*

Ephesians 5:20

*R*ichard Foster has written: "I had come to Kotzebue on the adventure of helping to 'build the first high school above the Arctic Circle,' but the work itself was far from an adventure. It was hard, backbreaking labor.

One day I was trying to dig a trench for a sewer line — no small task in a world of frozen tundra. An Eskimo man whose face and hands displayed the leathery toughness of many winters came by and watched me for a while. Finally he said simply and profoundly, 'You are digging a ditch to the glory of God.'

He said it to encourage me, I know. And I have never forgotten his words. Beyond my Eskimo friend no human being ever knew or cared whether I dug that ditch well or poorly. In time it was to be covered up and forgotten. But because of my friend's words, I dug with all my might, for every shovel-full of dirt was a prayer to God.

Even though I did not know it at the time, I was attempting in my small and unsophisticated way to do what the great artisans of the Middle Ages did when they carved the back of a piece of art, knowing that God alone would see it."[130]

When life gets tough, our tendency is to ask the Lord to change our circumstances. Perhaps we should ask him to change our outlook instead.

A single grateful thought raised to heaven is the most perfect prayer.

Praise the LORD!
Oh, give thanks to the LORD,
for He is good!
For His mercy endures forever.
Psalm 106:1 NKJV

$\mathcal{A}$lthough they may not have known the title of the painting, or the name of its painter, almost everyone has seen a copy of "The Song of the Lark," a famous painting by the French artist Jules Breton.

The painting depicts a peasant girl on her way to the field for a hard day's work. Suddenly, it appears, she has heard the sound of a lark. Breton captures her upturned face, alive with hope and joy, thrilled to hear the lilting beauty of the lark's sweet song. From her dress, she obviously is just another peasant girl with a difficult, work-a-day life. But Breton captures something of her inner soul — a human being glorying in one of nature's loveliest voices, a person enriched by the beauty of God's creation.

The painting has no image of a bird in it. The lark that gives rise to such pleasure is unseen.[131]

And so it is with our Christian walk. We do not see with our physical eyes the One with whom we walk and to whom we pray. Even so, it is He who gives our lives meaning. His words of comfort, admonition, encouragement, and direction prompt us to look upward with thanksgiving and praise.

Have you heard the song He is singing especially to *you* today?

No day is well spent without communication with God.

Evening, and morning, and at noon, will I pray, and cry aloud: and he shall hear my voice.

Psalm 55:17

A father and his daughter had a very close relationship and they spent a great deal of time in each other's company. Then one day, the father noticed a change in his daughter's behavior. If he suggested they go for a walk, she excused herself from going. If he offered an ice cream treat at a nearby soda shop, she declined the offer, but encouraged him to go on. If he said he was about to drive through the countryside on errands — an activity she had dearly loved — she gave some reason why she couldn't go.

The father grieved her absence, and although he searched his heart and memory for an incident which might have breached their relationship, he could find no reason for her behavior.

When his birthday came, she proudly presented him with a pair of exquisitely knitted slippers, saying, "I made these by myself, just for you." In that moment, he understood where she had been for the past three months. He said to her, "My darling, I like these slippers very much, but next time, let me buy slippers so I can spend with you all the hours you worked on them. I would rather have the joy of your company than anything you can make for me."[132]

So it is with our Heavenly Father. He much prefers the pleasure of our presence, than any works or good deeds we might present to Him.

He who runs from God
in the morning
will scarcely find Him
the rest of the day.

*Let me see your kindness
to me in the morning,
for I am trusting you.
Show me where to walk,
for my prayer is sincere.*

Psalm 143:8 TLB

$\mathcal{T}$he wife of a dairy farmer habitually rose at 4:30 each morning to milk their cows. When she recognized the need to begin each morning with prayer, she began rising thirty minutes earlier to pray before going to the barn. "Just made a startling discovery!" she wrote in her journal shortly after starting this practice. "The time on my knees each morning is the *preparation* for prayer. The rest of the day then *becomes* the prayer."

The great Christian doctor Paul Tournier had a similar experience with prayer. Determined to have a time of prayer before his early rounds, he went to his study, took out his pocket watch, and sat down. He planned to commit an hour to prayer. After a few minutes, he opened his eyes and discovered only a few minutes had elapsed! The next time he looked at his watch, it had been only a few more minutes.

Finally, the hour was over. He was disappointed that he had felt nothing during his prayer time. As he prepared to rise from his desk, he had an impulse to remain seated for a few more moments. He said it was in those moments, that God visited his heart. He was convinced that God had used the hour to test his obedience; the reward came in the brief time that followed.[133]

In the morning,
prayer is the key
that opens to us
the treasures of God's
mercies and blessings;
in the evening, it is the
key that shuts us up
under His protection
and safeguard.

*You have put gladness in my heart
...I will both lie down in peace,
and sleep; for You alone, O Lord,
make me dwell in safety.*

Psalm 4:7,8 NKJV

$\mathcal{F}$or several nights, a little girl threw one shoe under her bed before climbing into it for the night. Her mother asked her why. "Teacher said," the girl replied, "that if we have to kneel by our beds to look for our shoes, we'll remember to say our morning prayers while we're there."

The habit of early morning prayer has been kept by many notable Christian leaders, including the great evangelist Billy Sunday. Shortly after Billy was converted and joined the church, a Christian man put his arm on the young man's shoulder and said, "William, there are three simple rules I can give to you, and if you will hold to them, you will never write 'backslider' after your name.

"Take fifteen minutes each day to listen to God talking to you. Take fifteen minutes each day to talk to God. Take fifteen minutes each day to talk to others about God."

The young convert was deeply impressed and he determined to make those three things the foremost disciplines of his Christian life. From that day onward, throughout his life he spent the first minutes of every day alone with God and His Word. Before he read a letter, looked at a paper, or even read a telegram, he went first to the Bible, so that the first word he received for the day would be directly from God.[134]

Prayer should be the key of the morning and the bolt of the night.

■ ■ ■

O Lord, the God of my salvation,
I have cried to You for help by day;
at night I am in Your presence.

Psalm 88:1 AMP

*D*ennis Hamm has noted the "examen," or examination of conscience, is an ancient practice among Christians. In the early days of the church, the examen was a time for confession. Specifically, it was a process of examining one's daily behavior against the criteria of the Ten Commandments. Hamm proposes five practices that can help a person examine his or her day in prayer:

1. *Pray for light.* Ask God to give you illumination to help you see God's plan in the buzzing confusion of your day.

2. *Review the day in thanksgiving.* Think of the past 24 hours as a beautiful gift from the Lord. Walk through your day, hour to hour, thanking God for each task He gave you, each person He allowed you to encounter.

3. *Review the feelings that surface as you replay your day.* Both positive and negative feelings are signals to you about your own spiritual state. Let all of your feelings flow to the surface of your conscious mind.

4. *Take one of the feelings that surfaces (positive or negative) and pray from it.* You may be led to praise, petition, repentance, or a cry for helping or healing.

5. *Finally, look toward tomorrow.* What feelings do you have about the tasks and appointments that lie ahead? Whatever you are feeling, ask for God's help.[135]

Good endings come from prayerful beginnings.

My help comes from the Lord,
who made heaven and earth.

Psalm 121:2 NRSV

*O*ne day when Dwight L. Moody was preaching at a church in England, he felt an iciness in the congregation which he could not melt. He left the pulpit feeling leaden and stolid. The Spirit had not moved. All afternoon, Moody dreaded returning to preach the evening service. However, something dramatic happened in the evening service. It began with a look of warmth on a single face, then it spread. Moody felt, and saw it surging like a tide on the faces of the people before him. There was a great outpouring of the Spirit and crowds of people streamed into the aisles to accept Christ.

The people begged Moody to stay on. He promised to return to them after an engagement in Scotland. Upon his return, he heard what had happened.

Moody called upon an invalid church member and discovered that she had read of his work and had been praying for months that God would send him to stir the smoldering coals of faith in her church. Her sister had returned home from church after Moody first preached and had told her about the service. She was astonished that he had come. All afternoon and evening, she fasted and prayed for revival. Moody was convinced that she, had single-handedly been responsible for the dramatic change between the morning and evening services.[136]

God can use the faithful prayers of one person to release the warmth of His presence into many cold hearts, melting away their resistance and stirring the smoldering coals in their hearts.

Our Father which art in heaven,
Hallowed be thy name.
Thy kingdom come.
Thy will be done in earth,
as it is in heaven.
Give us this day our daily bread.
And forgive us our debts,
as we forgive our debtors.
And lead us not into temptation,
but deliver us from evil:
For thine is the kingdom,
and the power, and the glory,
for ever. Amen.

The Lord's Prayer
Matthew 6:9-13

𝑒very day throughout her childhood, a young woman ended her day by sitting on the edge of her bed with her mother and reciting the Lord's Prayer. After her "amen," her mother would add, "And dear God, bless..." and proceed to call out the names of numerous family members and friends, even people they had read about or heard about in the news.

Years passed. Then the little girl, now a mother with two daughters of her own, went on vacation to visit her in-laws. As a treat, the girls were allowed to stay up late. By eleven o'clock all the adults were exhausted and prepared for bed. Her youngest daughter, however, refused to budge. Not wanting the evening to end, she screamed, "no, no, no" and sat down in the middle of the hallway.

Suddenly, the mother recalled her prayer times with her mother. She picked up her daughter, who protested all they way, and carried her to her bedroom for the night. Sitting on the edge of the bed with her, she began to pray, "Our Father, who art in heaven...." and her daughter joined in. They finished their prayer with a long list of "God blesses." In fact, the little girl fell asleep right in the middle of one of her requests![137]

*O Lord, heavenly Father,
in whom is the fullness of light
and wisdom, enlighten our minds
by Your Holy Spirit, and give us
grace to receive Your Word with
reverence and humility, without
which no one can understand
Your truth.... Amen.*

—John Calvin

$\mathcal{A}$ longing for God's wisdom must always be coupled with reverence and understanding for justice, as this statement from the St. Hilda Community attests:

> As one who travels in the heat longs for cool waters, so do I yearn for wisdom;
> and as one who is weary with walking, so shall I sit at her well and drink.
>
> For her words are like streams in the desert; she is like rain on parched ground, like a fountain whose waters fail not.
> Whoever hears her voice will be content with nothing less; and whoever drinks of her will long for more.
>
> But who can find wisdom's dwelling place, and who has searched her out?
> For many have said to me, lo, here is wisdom, and there you shall find understanding; here is true worship of God, and thus shall your soul be satisfied.
>
> But there was no delight in my soul; all my senses were held in check.
> My body became alien to me, and my heart was shriveled within me.
> For I sought understanding without justice; discernment without the fear of God.[138]

*O Lord, You are never weary of
doing me good. Let me never be
weary of doing You service. But as
You have pleasure in the prosperity
of Your servants, so let me take
pleasure in the service of my Lord,
and abound in Your work, and in
Your love and praise evermore.
O fill up all that is wanting,
reform whatever is amiss in me,
perfect the thing that concerns me.
Let the witness of Your pardoning
love ever abide in my heart.*

—*John Wesley*

$\mathscr{I}$n an old book titled *Prevailing Prayer*, the author describes John Wesley's prayer life this way:

"As a matter of habit and rule, John Wesley's ordinary private praying consumed two hours a day. At times he would gather his company and pray all night, or till the power of God came down. Nothing was considered too great or too small to take to the Lord. Seized with a pain in the midst of his preaching, so that he could not speak, 'I know my remedy,' he says, and immediately kneeled down. In a moment the pain was gone, and the voice of the Lord cried aloud to sinners. Being seized with a pain, fever and cough, so that he could scarcely speak, 'I called on Jesus aloud to increase my faith. While I was speaking my pain vanished away, my fever left me, and my bodily strength returned.'

"Wesley moved things mightily, because he moved God mightily. He became the prince of evangelists, because he was the prince of prayers. He stirred the world with the fire of his zeal, because he had stirred heaven by the fire of his prayers. His pleas had access to men's consciences, because they had access to God."

May our lives be marked by such fervor in prayer!

Before I lay me down to sleep,
I give myself to Christ to keep.
Four corners to my bed,
four Angels overspread;
One at the head, one at the feet,
and two to guard me while I sleep.
I go by sea, I go by land,
the Lord made me with His right hand.
If any danger come to me,
sweet Jesus Christ, deliver me.
He is the branch and I'm the flower,
may God send me a happy hour.

—Traditional Bedtime Prayer

A sensitive, timid boy was accustomed to lying down to sleep in his bed, and then listening to the voices of his parents in their lighted sitting-room across the hallway. To him, it seemed that his parents never slept, for he left them awake when he was put to bed at night, and he found them awake when he left his bed in the morning. This thought brought him comfort since he often imagined monsters in the darkness of his room.

Just to make certain his strong father was standing guard, however, he had a habit, night after night, of calling out to his father, "Are you there, Papa?" The answer would come back cheerily, "Yes, son, I'm here."

"You'll take care of me tonight, Papa, won't you?" was the next question. "Yes, I'll take care of you, son," was the comforting response. "Go to sleep now. Good night." Assured of his father's care, the little boy would fall asleep.

The routine meant little to the father, but much to the son. Years later, himself a father and grandfather, he still calls out to his Heavenly Father each night, "Father, you'll take care of me tonight, won't You?" And the Father always answers back, "He that keepeth thee will not slumber" (Psalm 121:3).[139]

*Lord, make me an
instrument of Your peace;
where there is hatred, let me sow love;
where there is injury, pardon;
where there is doubt, faith;
where there is despair, hope;
where there is darkness, light;
where there is sadness, joy.
O Divine Master, grant that I may
not so much seek to be consoled, as to
console; to be understood, as to
understand; to be loved, as to love;
for it is in giving that we receive,
it is in pardoning that we are
pardoned, it is in dying that
we are born to eternal life.*

—St. Francis of Assisi

Francis' father brought him before the bishop of the diocese, wanting Francis to renounce all claims and return his goods. Because of his love for poverty, Francis readily agreed to go before the bishop. With no urging, hesitation, justification, or speech he took off his clothes and gave them to his father. As he disrobed it was revealed that he had on a hairshirt under his costly robes. In his zeal, he even took off his pants, so he stood naked before the bishop.

Francis said to his father, "Up to today I called you father but now I can say in all honesty, *Our Father who art in heaven*. He is my patrimony and I put my faith in Him."

The bishop was dumbstruck at Francis' zeal. He jumped up to embrace Francis and covered him with his own cape. He called his servants to bring him some clothes, one garment being an old smock that had belonged to a farmer. After drawing a cross on it with a piece of chalk, Francis put it on. He judged it a worthy garment for a follower of the crucified Christ. Thus, Francis, stripped of all possessions, felt he could now follow his Lord completely. Free of all earthly bonds, he left the town and sought for quiet places where he could be alone to hear the secrets God might reveal to him.[140]

May the strength of God pilot us.
May the power of God preserve us.
May the wisdom of God instruct us.
May the hand of God protect us.
May the way of God direct us.
May the shield of God defend us.
May the host of God guard us
—against the snares of the evil ones.
—against temptations of the world.
May Christ be with us!
May Christ be before us!
May Christ be in us,
Christ be over all!
May thy salvation, Lord, always be ours,
This day, O Lord, and evermore.

—Attributed to St. Patrick

$\mathcal{W}$hile skiing in Colorado one day, a man noticed some people on the slope wearing red vests. Moving closer, he could read these words on their vests: BLIND SKIER. The statement intrigued him. He had difficulty skiing with 20/20 vision! How could people without sight manage to ski?

He watched the skiers for awhile, and discovered the secret. Each skier had a guide who skied beside, behind, or in front of him, but always in a place where the two could easily communicate. The guide used two basic forms of communication. First, tapping the ski poles together to assure the blind person that he was there, and second, speaking simple, specific directions: "Go right. Turn left. Slow. Stop. Skier on your right."

For his part, the skier had the responsibility to trust the guide to speak for his good, and to immediately and completely obey the guide's instructions.[141]

We can't see even five seconds into the future. We cannot see the struggles to come, other people who may run into us, or we into them, like errant skiers on a crowded slope. But God has given us the Holy Spirit to be our Guide through life — to walk before and behind us, and to dwell in us. It is our role to listen and to obey.

Dear Jesus,
Help us to spread Your
fragrance everywhere we go.
Flood our souls with Your
Spirit and life. Penetrate
and possess our whole being
so utterly that our lives may be
a radiance of Yours...Let us
thus praise You in the way
You love best by shining on
those around us. Let us preach
You without preaching, not by
words, but by example by the
catching force, the sympathetic
influence of what we do,
the evident fullness of the love
our hearts bear to You.

—*Mother Teresa*

$\mathcal{M}$illions of people around the world consider Mother Teresa to be one of the most saintly Christians of this century. Few, however, know the lesson of her life.

Mother Teresa was born in 1910 as Agnes Gonxha Bojaxhiu in Skopje, Macedonia, of Albanian ancestry. At the age of 18, she traveled to Ireland to join the Institute of the Blessed Virgin Mary. Barely six weeks later, a novice in the ways of the church and of life, she was sent to India to be a teacher. She studied nursing there and soon moved into the slums of Calcutta, home to some of the most destitute people in the world. She felt especially drawn to the blind, the aged, lepers, the disabled, and the dying. She organized schools and opened centers to treat those whom no one else would touch, much less nurse. Under her guidance, a leper colony called "Town of Peace" (Shanti Naga) was built. In 1950, she founded the Order of the Missionaries of Charity, a congregation of women dedicated to help the poor.

Trained as a nurse, Mother Teresa has lived her life *as* a nurse, trusting that as she did her work, the Great Physician might do His work in her and through her.[142]

In whatever career you are pursuing today, you can trust the Lord to do His work in and through *you*.

*I kneel before the Father,
from whom the whole family
in heaven and on earth derives
its name. I pray that out of His
glorious riches He may strengthen
you with power through His Spirit
in your inner being, so that Christ
may dwell in your hearts through
faith. And I pray that you, being
rooted and established in love, may
have power, together with all the
saints, to grasp how wide and long
and high and deep is the love of
Christ, and to know this love that
surpasses knowledge — that you
may be filled to the measure of
all the fulness of God.*

■ ■ ■

*—Paul's Prayer for the Ephesians
(Paraphrased) Ephesians 3:14-19*

$\mathcal{T}$he Bible — carefully read and well-worn — was the most important book in Gerrit's house. His home was a house of prayer, where many tears were shed for revival in his church in Heemstede. Almost a generation later, his prayers were answered as that very church became the center of an upsurge of faith in Holland, part of the Great Awakening in Europe.

When Gerrit's great-granddaughter was about 18 years old, she had a dream about him. He was walking through a beautiful park with her and he said, "When you sow some seed and put it in the ground, this seed will make a plant, and this plant will give seed again.... You, my dear Corrie, are the daughter of my grandson.... You are a plant, blooming from my seed. I will show you something that will never be changed. It is the Word of God." In the dream, he opened his Bible and said, "This book will be the same forever." He then told her, "Plant the seeds from God's Book, and they will grow from generation to generation."

Corrie ten Boom did just that. She planted God's Word in hearts and minds around the world. Information learned in textbooks is continually updated. Courses of study change. The truths of the Bible, however, are absolutes. Its promises are sure.

God bless all those that I love;
God bless all those that love me;
God bless all those that love those
that I love and all those that love
those that love me.

—Sixteenth Century
New England Sampler

*C*onsider these three prayers for friends:

Dear God, Lover of us all, do not let me go down into the grave with old broken friendships unresolved. Give to us and to all with whom we have shared our lives and deepest selves along the Way, the courage not only to express anger when we feel let down, but Your more generous love which always seeks to reconcile and so to build a more enduring love between those we have held dear as friends. — Kathy Keay

Let us pray for our friends, that they may lead happy and useful lives. Let us pray for any friends with whom we have quarreled, that we may have the chance to be reconciled. Let us pray for those who are living in new surroundings and lack friends. Let us pray for those who have lost their friends by the way they live. Let us pray for those who befriend the friendless. God our Father, make us true and loyal friends. Grant that all our friends may lead us nearer You. — Caryl Micklem

Send down the dew of Thy heavenly grace upon us, that we may have joy in each other that passeth not away; and, having lived together in love here...may live for ever together with them, being made one in thee, in thy glorious kingdom hereafter. — John Austin[144]

References

Unless otherwise indicated, all Scripture quotations are taken from the *King James Version* of the Bible.

Scripture quotations marked NIV are taken from the *Holy Bible, New International Version®* NIV®. Copyright © 1973, 1978, 1984 by International Bible Society. Used by permission of Zondervan Publishing House. All rights reserved.

Scripture quotations marked NASB are taken from the *New American Standard Bible*. Copyright © The Lockman Foundation 1960, 1962, 1963, 1968, 1971, 1972, 1973, 1975, 1977. Used by permission.

Verses marked TLB are taken from *The Living Bible*, copyright © 1971. Used by permission of Tyndale House Publishers, Inc., Wheaton, Illinois 60189. All rights reserved.

Scripture quotations marked AMP are taken from *The Amplified Bible, Old Testament*, copyright © 1965, 1987 by Zondervan Corporation, Grand Rapids, Michigan. *New Testament* copyright © 1958, 1987 by The

Acknowledgments

Oswald Chambers (8), Henri Nouwen (10,126), Eliza M. Hickok (14), Lorrie Morgan (16), Robert South (18), Alexander Maclaren (30), Abraham Joshua Heschel (34), Francis Fenelon (36), Frederick Buechner (38), Thomas Brooks (40,42,44), Martin Luther (46,222, 260), G. Ashton Oldham (48), Joseph Fort Newton (50), Leonard Ravenhill (52), Charles L. Allen (54), Charles Spurgeon (56), George Failing (58), William McGill (62), Alexander Whyte (64), Ambrose (72), Thomas Fuller (76), Dorothy Thompson (78), Teresa of Avila (80), Hosea Ballou (82), Montaigne (84), William Poole (86), Thomas Hooker (88), James Montgomery (90), Julian of Norwich (94), Richard C. Trench (96), James O. Fraser (98), Reginald Johnson (100), Soren Kierkegaard (102), George E. Rees (104), William Cary (106), John Bunyan (108,122,268), Hannah More (110,164), George Appleton (112), O. Hallesby (114), Andrew Murray (118,128,246), Samuel Osgood (128), W.E. Sangster and Leslie Davison (136), Merlin R. Carothers (142), Peter Deyneka (144), Jack Hayford (148), Edward P. Roe (150), Madam De Gasparin (152), D.L. Moody (154), John Aikman Wallace (158), Julius

Hare (162), Jean Ingelow (166), Joseph Hall (168), Mark Hopkins (170), Rabbi Judah Halevi (174), John Calvin (178,290), Alfred Lord Tennyson (180), Lord Samuel (184), Bernard (186), Wesley L. Duewel (192,230), Clement of Alexandria (194), Henry Ward Beecher (196), John Owen (198), Richard Monckton Milnes (202), Louis Cassels (204), Mother Teresa (206,304), Sir William Gurney Benham (208), Phillips Brooks (214), Billy Graham (216,218), Joanna Baillie (220), Abraham Lincoln (222), Janette Oke (226), Dietrich Bonhoeffer (228), Corrie ten Boom (232), Austin Phelps (234), Robert Hall (240), John F. D. Maurice (248), Vance Havner (250), Samuel Taylor Coleridge (254), Sidlow Baxter (256), Charlotte Elliott (258), Victor Hugo (264), Archbishop Fulton Sheen (266), Gotthold Ephraim Lessing (274), John Wesley (292), St. Francis of Assisi (296,298), St. Patrick (300,302).

Endnotes

[1]*On the Anvil*, Max Lucado, (Wheaton, IL: Tyndale House, 1985) pp. 21,22.

[2]*Encourage Me*, Charles R. Swindoll, (Grand Rapids, MI: Zondervan, 1982) p. 61.

[3]*Encyclopedia of Sermon Illustrations*, David F. Burgess, ed. (St. Louis, MO: Concordia Publishing House, 1984), #741 and #318.

[4]*The Guideposts Handbook of Prayer*, Phyllis Hobe, ed. (Carmel, NY: Guideposts, 1982), pp. 49,50.

[5]*Illustrations Unlimited*, James S. Hewett, ed. (Wheaton, IL: Tyndale House, 1988), p. 419.

[6]*Encyclopedia of 7700 Illustrations*, Paul Lee Tan, ed. (Rockville, MD: Assurance Publishers, 1979), #4532.

[7]*Guideposts*, July, 1995, p. 12.

[8]*Inspirational Study Bible*, Max Lucado, ed. (Dallas, TX: Word, 1995), p. 1299.

[9]*Encyclopedia of 7700 Illustrations*, Paul Lee Tan, ed. (Rockville, MD: Assurance Publishers, 1979), #4535.

[10]*America*, August 26, 1995, p. 16.

[11]*Encyclopedia of 7700 Illustrations*, Paul Lee Tan, ed. (Rockville, MD: Assurance Publishers, 1979), #4564.

[12]*Guideposts*, October, 1995, p. 31.

[13]*Knight's Master Book of 4,000 Illustrations*, Walter B. Knight (Grand Rapids, MI: Eerdmans, 1956), p. 493.

[14]*Encyclopedia of 7700 Illustrations*, Paul Lee Tan, ed. (Rockville, MD: Assurance Publishers, 1979), #4589.

[15]*To Pray and To Love*, Robert Bondi (Minneapolis, MN: Fortress Press, 1991), p. 57.

[16]*Encyclopedia of Sermon Illustrations*, David F. Burgess, ed. (St. Louis, MO: Concordia Publishing House, 1984), p. 159.

[17]*Illustrations Unlimited*, James Hewett, ed. (Wheaton, IL: Tyndale House, 1988), pp. 418,419.

[18]*A Closer Walk*, Catherine Marshall (Old Tappan, NJ: Chosen Books (Fleming H. Revell), 1986), p. 162.

[19]*A Slow and Certain Light*, Elisabeth Elliot (Waco, TX: Word Books, 1973), p. 25.

[20]*Inspirational Study Bible*, Max Lucado, ed. (Dallas, TX: Word, 1995), pp. 188,189.

[21]*Encyclopedia of Sermon Illustrations*, David F. Burgess, ed. (St. Louis, MO: Concordia Publishing House, 1984), #740.

[22]*The Guideposts Handbook of Prayer*, Phyllis Hobe (Carmel, NY: Guideposts, 1982), p. 47.

[23]*Inspirational Study Bible,* Max Lucado, ed. (Dallas, TX: Word, 1995), pp. 330,331.

[24]*Too Busy Not To Pray*, Bill Hybels (Downers Grove, IL: InterVarsity Press, 1988), pp. 9,10.

[25]*American Health*, a Reader's Digest publication, June, 1995, pp. 131,133.

[26]*With Justice for All*, John Perkins (Ventura, CA: Regal Books (GL Publications), 1982), pp. 97-101.

[27]*Encyclopedia of 7700 Illustrations*, Paul Lee Tan, ed. (Rockville, MD: Assurance Publishers, 1979), #4660.

[28]*Decision*, September, 1995, p. 33.

[29]*Born Again*, Charles Colson (NY: Bantam Books, 1977), pp. 390-392.

[30]*Encyclopedia of 7700 Illustrations*, Paul Lee Tan, ed. (Rockville, MD: Assurance Publishers, 1979), #4538.

31*The Table of Inwardness*, Calvin Miller (Downers Grove, IL: InterVarsity Press, 1984), p. 90.

32*They Walked With God*, James S. Bell, Jr., ed. (Chicago: Moody Press, 1993).

33*Encyclopedia of 7700 Illustrations*, Paul Lee Tan, ed. (Rockville, MD: Assurance Publishers, 1979), #4584.

34*Mourning Into Dancing*, Walter Wangerin, Jr. (Grand Rapids, MI: Zondervan, 1992), pp. 266-268.

35*Illustrations for Preaching & Teaching*, Craig Brian Larson, ed. (Grand Rapids, MI: Baker Books, 1993), #171.

36*Guideposts*, July, 1995, p. 5.

37*My Utmost for His Highest*, Oswald Chambers (Grand Rapids, MI: Discovery House Publishers, 1992).

38*Encyclopedia of 7700 Illustrations*, Paul Lee Tan, ed. (Rockville, MD: Assurance Publishers, 1979), #4634.

39*The Guideposts Handbook of Prayer*, Phyllis Hobe (Carmel, NY: Guideposts, 1982), p. 72.

40*Beyond Ourselves*, Catherine Marshall, (Carmel, NY: Guideposts, 1961), pp. 72-74.

41*A Moment a Day*, Mary Beckwith & Kathi Mills (Ventura, CA: Regal Books, 1968), pp. 220,221.

42*Wisdom of the Saints*, Jill Haak Adels (NY: Oxford University Press, 1987), p. 40.

43*Encyclopedia of 7700 Illustrations*, Paul Lee Tan, ed. (Rockville, MD: Assurance Publications, 1979), #4639.

44*Too Busy Not To Pray*, Bill Hybels (Downers Grove, IL: InterVarsity Press, 1988), pp. 44,45.

45*And the Angels Were Silent*, Max Lucado (NY: Walker and Co., 1992), p. 13.

[46]*Encyclopedia of 7700 Illustrations*, Paul Lee Tan, ed. (Rockville, MD: Assurance Publications, 1979), #4553 and #4554.

[47]*The Christian Speaker's Treasury*, Ruth A. Tucker (NY: Harper & Row Publishers, San Francisco, 1989), pp. 269,270.

[48]*Encyclopedia of 7700 Illustrations*, Paul Lee Tan, ed. (Rockville, MD: Assurance Publishers, 1979), #4572.

[49]*Decision*, April, 1996, p. 12.

[50]*Teach Us How To Pray*, Louis Evely, Trans. Edmond Bonin (NY: Newman Press, 1967), p. 3.

[51]*Three Steps Forward, Two Steps Back*, Charles R. Swindoll (Nashville, TN: Thomas Nelson, 1980), p. 80.

[52]*Life in the Spirit*, Mother Teresa, Kathryn Spink, ed. (San Francisco, Harper & Row, 1983), p. 19.

[53]*Encyclopedia of 7700 Illustrations*, Paul Lee Tan, ed. (Rockville, MD: Assurance Publishers, 1979), #4573.

[54]*Trusting God in a Twisted World*, Elisabeth Elliot (Old Tappan, NJ: Fleming H. Revell Co., 1989), pp. 30,31.

[55]*Bread for the Wilderness, Wine for the Journey*, John Killinger, (Waco, TX: Word Books, 1976), pp. 128,129.

[56]*Wisdom of the Saints*, Jill Haak Adels (NY: Oxford University Press, 1987), p. 39.

[57]*Encyclopedia of 7700 Illustrations*, Paul Lee Tan, ed. (Rockville, MD: Assurance Publishers, 1979), #4587.

[58]*Guideposts*, April, 1996, p. 31.

[59]*He Still Moves Stones*, Max Lucado (Dallas, TX: Word Publishing, 1993), pp. 148,149.

[60]*Encyclopedia of 7700 Illustrations*, Paul Lee Tan, ed. (Rockville, MD: Assurance Publishers, 1979), #4655.

[61]*The Spiritual Art of Creative Silence*, Jeanie Miley (Wheaton, IL: Harold Shaw Publishers, 1989, 1996), pp. 151,152.

[62]*It's My Turn*, Ruth Bell Graham (Minneapolis: Grason, 1982), pp. 165,166.

[63]*Encyclopedia of 7700 Illustrations*, Paul Lee Tan, ed. (Rockville, MD: Assurance Publishers, 1979), #1918.

[64]*The Pursuit of Holiness*, Jerry Bridges (Colorado Springs, CO: NavPress, 1978, 1996), p. 128.

[65]*Diamonds in the Dust*, Joni Eareckson Tada (Grand Rapids, MI: Zondervan, 1993).

[66]*Encyclopedia of 7700 Illustrations*, Paul Lee Tan, ed. (Rockville, MD: Assurance Publishers, 1979), #4578.

[67]*Adventures in Prayer*, Catherine Marshall (Old Tappan, NJ: Chosen Books (Fleming Revell), 1975), pp. 24,25.

[68]*The Secret Kingdom*, Pat Robertson (Dallas, TX: Word Publishing, 1992), pp. 237-239.

[69]*Encyclopedia of 7700 Illustrations*, Paul Lee Tan, ed. (Rockville, MD: Assurance Publishers, 1979), #4539 and #4540.

[70]*Storm Warning*, Billy Graham (Dallas, TX: Word Publishing, 1992), pp. 51-53.

[71]*Encyclopedia of 7700 Illustrations*, Paul Lee Tan, ed. (Rockville, MD: Assurance Publishers, 1979), #4555.

[72]*The Spiritual Art of Creative Silence*, Jeanie Miley (Wheaton, IL: Harold Shaw Publishers, 1989, 1996), pp. 143,144.

[73]*Inspirational Study Bible,* Max Lucado, ed. (Dallas: Word, 1995), p. 1376.

[74]*Diamonds in the Dust*, Joni Eareckson Tada (Grand Rapids, MI: Zondervan, 1993).

[75]*Encyclopedia of 7700 Illustrations*, Paul Lee Tan, ed. (Rockville, MD: Assurance Publishers, 1979), #4590 and #4592.

[76]*Keep a Quiet Heart*, Elisabeth Elliot (Ann Arbor, MI: Servant Publications, 1995), p. 185.

[77]*Illustrations Unlimited*, James S. Hewett, ed. (Wheaton, IL: Tyndale House, 1988), pp. 428,429.

[78]*Encyclopedia of 7700 Illustrations*, Paul Lee Tan, ed. (Rockville, MD: Assurance Publishers, 1979), #4537.

[79]*The Power and Blessing*, Jack Hayford, (Wheaton, IL: Victor Books (Scripture Press Publications, Inc.), 1994), p. 232.

[80]*Three Steps Forward, Two Steps Back*, Charles R. Swindoll (Nashville, TN: Thomas Nelson, 1980), p. 75.

[81]*Encyclopedia of 7700 Illustrations*, Paul Lee Tan, ed. (Rockville, MD: Assurance Publishers, 1979), #4518, #4519.

[82]*Healing Words*, Larry Dossey, MD (NY: Harper Collins Publishers (HarperSan Francisco), 1993), pp. 179,180.

[83]*A Simple Path*, Mother Teresa (NY: Ballantine Books, 1995), pp. 7-10.

[84]*Encyclopedia of 7700 Illustrations*, Paul Lee Tan, ed. (Rockville, MD: Assurance Publishers, 1979), #4586.

[85]*Decision*, October, 1995, p. 23.

[86]*Encyclopedia of 7700 Illustrations*, Paul Lee Tan, ed. (Rockville, MD: Assurance Publishers, 1979), #4521.

[87]*It's My Turn*, Ruth Bell Graham (Minneapolis , MN: Grason, 1982), pp. 30-32.

[88]*A Moment a Day*, Mary Beckwith and Kathi Mills (Ventura, CA: Regal Books, 1988), pp. 199,120.

[89]*Healing Words*, Larry Dossey, MD (NY: HarperCollins Publishers (HarperSan Francisco), 1993), p. 209.

[90]*Illustrations Unlimited.* James S. Hewett, ed. (Wheaton, IL: Tyndale House, 1988), p. 416.

[91]*Encyclopedia of 7700 Illustrations*, Paul Lee Tan, ed. (Rockville, MD: Assurance Publishers, 1979), #4560.

[92]*They Walked With God*, James S. Bell, Jr., ed. (Chicago: Moody Press, 1993).

[93]*Encyclopedia of Sermon Illustrations*, David F. Burgess, ed. (St. Louis, MO: Concordia Publishing House, 1984), #735.

[94]*Decision*, June, 1996, p. 33.

[95]*The Christian Speaker's Treasury*, Ruth A. Tucker (NY: Harper & Row Publishers, San Francisco, 1989), pp. 145,146.

[96]*Encyclopedia of Sermon Illustrations*, David F. Burgess, ed. (St. Louis, MO: Concordia Publishing House, 1984), #728 and #731.

[97]Revised and rewritten from first-person testimonial found in *Guideposts*, July, 1996, pp. 32,33.

[98]*Inspirational Study Bible,* Max Lucado, ed. (Dallas: Word, 1995), p. 82.

[99]*Encyclopedia of 7700 Illustrations*, Paul Lee Tan, ed. (Rockville, MD: Assurance Publishers, 1979), #4596.

[100]*Decision*, April, 1996, p. 33.

[101]*Diamonds in the Dust*, Joni Eareckson Tada, (Grand Rapids, MI: Zondervan, 1993).

[102]*Wisdom of the Saints*, Jill Haak Adels, (NY: Oxford University Press, 1987), p. 40.

[103]*Knight's Treasury of 2,000 Illustrations*, Walter B. Knight (Grand Rapids, MI: Wm. B. Eerdmans Publishing Co., 1963), p. 491.

[104]*What Happens When We Pray for Our Families*, Evelyn Christenson (Wheaton, IL: Victor Books (Scripture Press Publications), 1992), pp. 13,14.

[105]*Illustrations Unlimited*, James S. Hewett, ed. (Wheaton, IL: Tyndale House, 1988), p. 428.

[106]*A Lamp for My Feet*, Elisabeth Elliot (Ann Arbor, MI: Servant Publications, 1987), p. 61.

[107]*Knight's Treasury of 2,000 Illustrations*, Walter B. Knight (Grand Rapids, MI: Wm. B. Eerdmans Publishing Co., 1963), pp. 250-252.

[108]*Guideposts*, August, 1995, p. 23.

[109]*Not I, But Christ*. Corrie ten Boom, (NY: Walker and Co., 1986), pp. 22-26.

[110]*Encyclopedia of 7700 Illustrations*, Paul Lee Tan, ed. (Rockville, MD: Assurance Publishers, 1979), #4574.

[111]*How To Listen to God*, Charles Stanley (Nashville, TN: Oliver Nelson (Thomas Nelson), 1985), p. 97.

[112]*Walking With Christ in the Details of Life*, Patrick M. Morley (Nashville: Thomas Nelson, 1992), pp. 59,60.

[113]*A Moment a Day*, Mary Beckwith and Kathi Mills (Ventura, CA: Regal Books, 1988), p. 468.

[114]*Trusting God in a Twisted World*, Elizabeth Elliot (Old Tappan, NJ: Fleming H. Revell Co., 1989), pp. 156,157.

[115]*The Body*, Charles Colson (Dallas: Word Publishing, 1992), pp. 212,213.

[116]*Encyclopedia of 7700 Illustrations*, Paul Lee Tan, ed. (Rockville, MD: Assurance Publishers, 1979), #4520.

[117]*Keep a Quiet Heart*, Elisabeth Elliot (Ann Arbor, MI: Servant Publications, 1995), p. 117.

[118]*Bread for the Wilderness, Wine for the Journey*, John Killinger (Waco, TX: Word Books, 1976), p. 44.

[119]*Christianity Today*, October 2, 1995, pp. 106,107.

[120]*Inspirational Study Bible,* Max Lucado, ed. (Dallas, TX: Word, 1995), pp. 196,197.

[121]*Encyclopedia of Sermon Illustrations*, David F. Burgess, ed. (St. Louis, MO: Concordia Publishing House, 1984), #739.

[122]*Encyclopedia of 7700 Illustrations*, Paul Lee Tan, ed. (Rockville, MD: Assurance Publishers, 1979), #4579.

[123]*Commonwealth*, December 1, 1995, p. 31.

[124]*Life in the Spirit*, Mother Teresa, Kathryn Spink, ed. (San Francisco: Harper & Row, 1983), pp. 76,77.

[125]*Encyclopedia of 7700 Illustrations*, Paul Lee Tan, ed. (Rockville, MD: Assurance Publishers, 1979), #4517.

[126]*Glorious Intruder*, Joni Eareckson Tada (Portland, OR: Multnomah Press, 1989), p. 192.

[127]*They Walked With God*, James S. Bell, Jr., ed. (Chicago: Moody Press, 1993).

[128]*Knight's Treasury of 2,000 Illustrations*, Walter B. Knight (Grand Rapids, MI: Wm. B. Eerdmans Publishing Co., 1963), p. 490.

[129]*The Pursuit of Holiness*, Jerry Bridges (Colorado Springs, CO: NavPress, 1978, 1996), pp. 24,25.

[130]*Seeking the Kingdom*, Richard J. Foster (San Francisco, CA: HarperSanFrancisco, 1995), p. 101.

[131]*Encyclopedia of 7700 Illustrations*, Paul Lee Tan, ed. (Rockville, MD: Assurance Publishers, 1979), #4638.

[132]*Unto the Hills*, Billy Graham (Waco, TX: Word Books, 1986), p. 158.

[133]*Bread for the Wilderness, Wine for the Journey*, John Killinger (Waco, TX: Word Books, 1976), pp. 66,67.

[134]*Encyclopedia of 7700 Illustrations*, Paul Lee Tan, ed. (Rockville, MD: Assurance Publishers, 1979), #4618 and #4558.

[135]*America*, May 14, 1994, pp. 22,23.

[136]*Bread for the Wilderness*, Wine for the Journey, John Killinger (Waco, TX: Word Books, 1976), pp. 91,92.

[137]*Guideposts*, July 1995, p. 41.

[138]*The Complete Book of Christian Prayers* (NY: Continuum Publishing Co., 1995), pp. 238,239.

[139]*Keep a Quiet Heart*, Elisabeth Elliot (Ann Arbor, MI: Servant Publications, 1995), pp. 229,230.

[140]*St. Francis of Assisi*, Lawrence Cunninghman (San Francisco: Harper & Row, Publishers, 1981), p. 28.

[141]*Hearing God*, Peter Lord (Grand Rapids, MI: Baker Book House, 1988), p. 18.

[142]*Compton's Encyclopedia*/America On Line.

[143]*The Complete Book of Christian Prayer* (NY: Continuum Publishing Co., 1995), pp. 84,85.

Additional copies of this book and other titles
in the *God's Little Devotional Book* series
are available at your local bookstore.

God's Little Devotional Book
God's Little Devotional Book for Couples
God's Little Devotional Book for Dads
God's Little Devotional Book for Graduates
God's Little Devotional Book for Men
God's Little Devotional Book for Mom
God's Little Devotional Book for Students
God's Little Devotional Book on Success
God's Little Devotional Book for Women

Honor Books
Tulsa, Oklahoma